FOLLOWING GOD
INTO THE
TRENCHES

The Effectiveness of Small Urban Church Ministry

By Dr. Michael D Wright Sr.

www.xulonpress.com

To
DONNa

May GOD Richly
Bless You

Ephesians
2: 8-9

PAstor

Mike

ACKNOWLEDGEMENTS

Although my name is on the cover of this book as its editor, the foundation and credit for this project from its inception to its fruition should be shared by several key people. First I want to give all glory and honor to my God and Jesus Christ my Lord and Savior, whom without I can do nothing. To my wife and ministry partner Lynne, who so lovingly and encouragingly believed God with me as we followed Jesus into the community, joining the Holy Spirit in the missional work of the Creator. Her encouragement and hard work in the development of this project is invaluable. Additional thanks to my daughter Latonya for her hard work and long hours in editing this manuscript. I would also like to thank the Christ Bible Fellowship Church of Philadelphia for following me into the trenches, and giving unselfishly to the work of the ministry. I want to give a special thanks to the Rev. Dr. David Grafton who encouraged me to write with excellency and purpose. Thank you for the many hours spent on editing this project and encouraging me to see it through. Lastly, but not least I would like to thank the Rev. Dr. Charles Leonard for allowing me opportunities to share my missional experience with his students which encouraged me to write this book.

TABLE OF CONTENTS

Introduction:

The Giants in Small Church Ministry

What this book is about

This book is designed to produce an image of the David and Goliath story in the minds of its readers that can be used for ministry. In this story the shepherd boy David was able to overcome a powerful giant named Goliath with five smooth stones through the power of God and strength of the Holy Spirit (1 Samuel 1:1-54). David as a mere shepherd boy tending his father's sheep, without any military training or experience, demonstrates to us size does not matter when we walk according to the will of God.

This book will detail one congregation's testimony as they learned to listen to, see, and follow God amidst the giants of society. This book will also encourage its readers through biblical data, biblical doctrine, and personal pastoral leadership serving in a small urban church. The author will provide proof that small urban churches can be effective despite the lack of a large numerical membership and the abundance of resources. The aim of this book is to strengthen small churches across the globe, helping others to understand that they too can overcome the giant mentality that bigger is better. The hope is that this research will enlighten larger churches as well and encourage them to support and strengthen the corner stone of Christianity called the small church.

Small Church dilemmas

Many small church ministries feel that because of their size and scarce resources they cannot be effective in restoring hope and positive change in their communities. This is especially true in the African American community in which the author serves.

Small church ministries have found themselves on the front lines without support, feeling inferior, facing a society lost and without hope. In small church settings we will discover that only a few people do all the work and therefore burnout happens frequently causing some to seek out larger congregations where the work load is shared. This study will explore how small church ministry, regardless of size, can yield to the Spirit and will of God, and can be used as an effective and vibrant tool in the hands of the Master. The small church possesses the ability to revitalize and bring restoration to urban communities across the globe. We must stay clear of all the rags to riches stories and come to understand revitalization does not always present itself in a mass restoration image. Restoration of urban communities often presents itself on many levels and in many ways.

Advantages of Small Churches

Because of the presence of small churches, the single mother with four children now has a church she can get to without a car. This church helps her to raise her children in the fear and admonition of the Lord. She now has a family after her biological family has given up on her. The small church assists her and provides the tools for raising her children while giving the family a sense of purpose and of belonging. The small church also gives her a human picture of Jesus in the community and her life.

What about the grandmother who is attempting to raise her grandchildren alone while the parents are no longer in the picture due to incarceration and or drug use? Because of the presence of the small urban church, she now has a support system that is close to her home and a part of her immediate community, this small community church understands her life and circumstances. She can even send the children to church, with its proximity within walking distance. Being able to send them will also give her a period of respite. To her the small church has restored hope, peace of mind and has become vital to her health and the life of her family.

What about the young man who has just been released from prison? To him the small church is a place of comfort, a place to belong, and a community that he is familiar with.

These are just a few examples of how a small church has restored hope and dignity in African American communities and others across the globe, and serves as a model for faithful ministry. It is our hope that this book will restore hope and dignity to the small church globally, but in particular the small urban church.

A Chronological View

Pastor Michael Wright and his wife Lynne received a call from the Lord to become church planters in the urban environment of Philadelphia, Pennsylvania. This call came with much tension and insecurity in the hearts and minds of this married couple who has spent their lives in this urban city. Pastor Mike and Lynne sought counsel from spiritual leaders, some who confirmed God's calling and others who felt that the timing was not right. However, Pastor Mike and Lynne continued to reject their calling for more than a year. Finally, after many sleepless nights, and through much prayer, this ministry couple yielded to the call of God to become independent church planters.

In February of 2003, Mike and Lynne opened up their home for prayer and Bible study. Within three months the Christ Bible Fellowship Church, also known as CBF, was born.

The small urban house church continued in prayers, biblical teaching and the preaching of God's word while the membership increased. Members began to tell other family members and friends about the small house church, and soon it became a growing church filled with families. CBF continued in the house setting for one year as the membership size continued to grow. The increased membership made it impossible to continue ministry in the small house church, and a bigger facility was needed.

In February 2004, the need for a larger facility was met by renting a storefront church in the heart of the Germantown section of Philadelphia. It was in this setting that the membership continued to outgrow its space. As the church continued to grow, the present space became insufficient. The ability to carry out ministries for adults and children was becoming increasingly difficult in the small storefront church. Over the next three years the membership declined due to the lack of space. The location was in a business district with restricted parking, which made it difficult for members to access without fear of cars being towed.

In August of 2007, Mike and Lynne received an invitation to fellowship with a church in the Kensington section of Philadelphia. This church was on the verge of closing its doors and was directed by the Lord to gift the entire church facility to Pastor Mike and his wife Lynne for the work of the ministry. This facility had more than enough space to grow and do ministry. With such a gracious and spacious gift Pastor Mike and Lynne were extremely grateful to God and the departing congregation but yet a bit perplexed, knowing that their membership had now dwindled down to eight members.

In September of 2007, the CBF congregation embarked on a journey to follow God into a community to join God's mission. This journey would grow them spiritually and test their faith in God, as they experienced God's power in the midst of sorrows, triumphs and the joy of being sent agents of Jesus Christ into a hurting and dying community. Join them as you experience the power of God in this congregation as they are challenged through fear and uncertainty, as they mature in Jesus Christ.

Chapter One

Biblical and Theological Foundations of Small Church Ministry

Biblical evidence of small church ministry

In this chapter we will explore biblical and theological foundations for small church ministry. It is our intention to provide biblical data and a historic evidence of the small church in its origins as it spreads throughout the biblical narrative. The small church is not unique to the 21st century urban and rural environments, but has been a cornerstone in the proliferation of Christianity.

We will examine the theology of the small church through Scripture and see how it has always been the apple of God's eyes, just like its larger counterpart. This study will provide a different lens in which to view the small church. The small church has always been a part of God's plan for humanity and continues to thrive in that plan today. We will discover how the small church transcends denominations, geography, social, and economic restraints. Its presence has always and will continue to be global. Not only will we examine the biblical theology of the small church, but we will review its function in the 21st century.

In order to find biblical evidence of small church ministry that would suffice for this model, we first need to define what constitutes a small church. How do we define the small church? Defining the small church has been a difficult task at best. There are many studies and ideas on what constitutes a small church. Narrowing it down to a singular concept requires lots of hard work and documented data, especially when we consider culture, socioeconomics, contexts, and denominations.

Therefore, there is no singular definition that would properly define the small church, and satisfy every denomination.

Jesus states "For where two or three are gathered together in My name, I am there in the midst of them (Matthew 18:20 NJKV)." Biblically speaking, two or three could constitute a small church. So we can easily understand from the words of Jesus that the definition of small church could easily apply to a certain number of gathered people.

Lyle E. Schaller in *Small Congregation: Big Potential* provides us a working definition and data to support a popular view of what a small church membership may look like. Schaller states "Many readers may prefer to define small American Protestant congregations as those averaging 100 or fewer at worship. That is a good round number and easy to defend. One reason to use it is, relatively few congregations averaging less than 100 at worship are served by a full-time and fully credentialed resident pastor." [1]

For the purpose of this study we will use 12-100 as a definition of small church ministry. This encompasses cultural, contextual, socioeconomic, and denominational diversity. It also gives us a base from the biblical text of the twelve disciples that Jesus called and commissioned to enlarge the church (Luke 9:1-6).

Small churches are effective in gospel proclamation throughout the urban spaces in North America. Furthermore, it includes the multitude of storefront churches found throughout the urban environment in major cities, and the rural landscapes of the Midwest. Small churches make up the global community of churches. It also encompasses the hidden church in the Middle East, the small church on the mid-western farm, or the church that meets faithfully in coffee shops eager for the word of the Lord.

Schaller defines small church in *The Small Church is Different* as "The small church is the normative institutional expression of the worshiping congregation among Protestant denominations on the North American continent.

One fourth of all Protestant congregations on this continent have fewer than thirty-five people in attendance at the principal weekly worship service, and one half averages less than seventy-five." [2] In Matthew 16:13-18, Jesus ask the disciples, the (12) "who do men say that I am?" After receiving several answers Jesus declares "It is upon this rock I will build my church." One could interpret that this particular church started with 12 congregational members known throughout the biblical text as disciples. If this is true, then we can extract from the text that this church of 12 could be considered a small church.

Jim Feeney in *"Small Churches Please God Too"* summarizes "Small churches far outnumber megachurches. The pastors and members of those small churches can wrongly develop an inferiority complex if they fail to realize God's great love for the small church and its treasured place in God's heart." [3]

Feeney examines the gospel of Luke 12:32 as the theological foundations and biblically- based evidence, of God's view towards the small church. Here he records Jesus as stating "Do not fear, little flock, for it is your Father's good pleasure to give you the kingdom (Luke 12:32 NKJV)." Feeney states "Little flock is an excellent expression to describe the thousands of dedicated small churches throughout the United States and the world. Jesus loved his own little flock of disciples, and God the Father was pleased to bless them." [4]

Feeney continues to state "God the Father takes great pleasure in the multitude of little flocks gathering in small church congregations, home fellowships, home Bible studies, prayer groups and the like.

The small church not only has a place in our society today, but has always been foundational in the global spreading of Christianity, from the persecution of those of "The Way" through the ascendance of Jesus Christ and the grand entrance of the Holy Spirit." [5]

In addition to the Gospels, we might look to the Epistles for an understanding of the small church. The Apostle Paul in 1 Corinthians 16:19 sends greetings from the churches of Asia and also from Aquila and Priscilla. The two were a 1st century married missionary couple who were overseers of a church in their home. Paul makes two distinctions that are worth taking a look at. Paul first identifies the gathering of those of "The Way" as a church. Secondly, Paul identifies where the church gathering was located, in the house of Priscilla and Aquila.

One can gather from the text that this was a small 1st century church. In the 1st century, even the wealthiest homes where those of "The Way" could have met, would have typically held 65-70 people.

Mario Barbero writes in A First-century Couple, Priscilla and Aquila: Their House Churches and Missionary Activity' "Aquila and Priscilla are not anonymous members of the community. They have faces and names. They send warm greetings. They are a link between the church of Corinth (which they helped start) and the churches of Asia. They have a community at their home; they are "church builders." [6]

We can readily identify this 1st century church with the 21st century urban churches today. The 1st century small churches were very popular for many reasons. These reasons included protection from persecution, mobility, central for evangelism, discipleship through example, and proclamation through the common meals. These same reasons are readily seen and acted out in our urban community churches today.

Kevin Giles in "House Churches," gives us an understanding that is often overlooked in the biblical text but lifted up through exegesis. Giles suggests: Because the house setting of church gatherings was self-evident and unquestionable, the New Testament writers did not take time to detail their makeup and history. One can assume that they might have thought, their readers would have been familiar with the house church and might have even attended such, therefore neglecting to give attention to detail about its design and operation." [7]

An example of this is clearly outlined in Acts 17:1-9. Here the Apostle Paul entered the synagogue in Thessalonica and reasoned from the Scriptures, causing an uproar. Fearing the mob, Jason then took Paul and Silas into his home to shelter them from the mob. Through exegesis one can suggest that in Jason's home (small church) Paul continued to reason from Scriptures.

Brandon O'Brien in *The Strategically Small Church* writes "Acts 2 records the birth of many small-even-micro-congregations.

The rest of Acts repeats this theme. Acts 9 tells us that it was not a single church that grew in numbers, but the church throughout Judea, Galilee, and Samaria. These small congregations did not meet in a single building.

They met in homes, synagogues, and public spaces. In the passages where Scripture records the increase of numbers, it is usually testifying to the growth of the church universal, not a single congregation."[8] The Bible flows with biblical evidence of small churches. We now have a theological foundation of small churches in the 1st century and throughout the New Testament text.

We must be careful not to assume that being small means that we do not have to grow. We can reference Acts 2:42-47 where the Lord added to the church daily those who were being saved. Growth is taking place through the New Testament text, but we can argue this on a universal level. In Matthew 28, the disciples were instructed to go and make disciples. This certainly has an element of growth, looking forward to the universal church in the future, and not necessarily local small churches into large churches. The intentionality of church growth has been incorporated in the Day of Pentecost. Acts 2:5-10 lets us know that they were visitors from different nations. Which suggests that they would have taken the gospel back to their land of origin, where worship would have occurred house to house, constituting a small church setting.

Small Churches in the 21st Century
Why are There Small Churches?

Despite biblical evidence of small churches and historical role of the small church in Christianity, many people still ask the question "why are there small churches?" Anthony G. Pappas in *Inside The Small Church* responds to this question, while dealing with the expert's view for the diminishment of small churches. Pappas states "The future of the small church is the subject of varied opinions. Church consultant Bill Easum claims that up to 75% of existing small churches will be closed before a half –century goes by. Kennon Callahan, another expert on congregational life, asserts that the small church will be one of four viable forms of the church into the foreseeable future."[9]

But Pappas answers "Indeed, 16,000 house churches have come into being in the last few years! These are small groups functioning as congregations. They have arrived on the scene almost entirely independently and spontaneously. Collectively, they represent 5% of congregations in the United States! While these are not the typical, mainline small church complete with building, by-laws, and tradition, their emergence bespeaks the soul's need for face-to-face spiritual experience." [10]

This need for personal interaction and face-to-face communication is one reason for the small church existence. This kind of fellowship is invaluable to those in need of personal touch and the extended family. For those who need this human interaction, it is like breath in the body. It also provides the opportunity for the minister to be in touch directly with lives of the members. Pappas gives several realities why there will be more small churches in the days ahead. He suggests that the current midsize church often seeks to return to their former status as the large congregation they once were. In an attempt to accomplish this former glory, they often drown for failure to tread water in a society with changing church trends.

Denominations also play a role in why small churches will continue in the days ahead. Denominations continue to allocate resources into starting satellite ministries and new churches, these churches are designed to function as small congregations. As denominations engage communities in the rebuilding process, small churches are being developed as a method for incarnational ministries.

Only a generation ago, combining two small and geographically close congregations was seen as good stewardship. Now it is known to be impossible!" [11]

Papas gives us just a few reasons why the small church exists and will continue to function as a viable part of the Body of Christ. The energy and ability to touch lives on a personal level gives it the life it needs to continue in a world where bigger is better. Its small size, allows for mobility to move and adapt to changes in climate such as buildings, finances, community changes, generational changes, and attacks from the evil one.

Maybe we should reverse the question and ask why are there large or mega churches? We have seen from the historical perspective that small churches have always been prevalent and foundational in the spreading of Christianity. Have we moved away from the norm and developed a "new norm" called the large church?

David Ray in *The Big Small Church Book* states "From the first century through the twentieth century, most churches have been small.

Sixty percent of the churches in America have fewer than seventy-five people in Sunday worship. Many more think and act like small churches. Small churches are the norm, primarily because many people still find them to be the right size in which to love God and their neighbor. It is expected they will continue to be the norm." [12]

Some people wonder why every congregation does not grow into large or mega congregation in the 21st century. There are assumptions that if a congregation does not reach a certain numerical criterion (critical mass) then it is not a real church. If one were to walk into any Christian bookstore in the United States of America, he or she would be sure to find a large concentration *"more than needed"* of books on church growth.

Some of the books one might find in local book stores are: Purpose Driven Church, There's Hope for Your Church, How to Spark Immediate Growth in Your Church, and The Church Growth Handbook.

Our culture has concentrated its evangelical thoughts on how to grow your church or how to increase its size. While there is nothing wrong with church growth, but a concentration on growth will often send the underlying message that there is something intrinsically wrong with the small church. Bigness becomes the ideal and any church that does not pursue numerical growth runs the risk of an inferiority complex.

Douglas C. May in the *Concordia Theological Quarterly* writes "Why, then, are there small congregations? My answer is that there are people who are separated from larger flocks by distance, language, or culture. There are small churches because these people are not served by the larger congregations.

These small churches are accessible and are able to bridge the gap that larger churches are not able to fill." [13] May goes on to say "Maybe it is because the Lord can accomplish things in small churches that is not done in larger churches.

The family atmosphere of the small church provides more support for the family structure." [14] May has a valid point that each church big or small has its uniqueness in the eyes of God, and has the ability to be used as an instrument in God's plans. They also served as extended families for those who have been shunned by their birth family and those without family.

Across the urban landscape in North America, one can find small storefront churches on any given corner in its urban spaces. Katie Day in *Faith on the Avenue* maps out over 80 churches that line the eight and a half miles of cobblestone and trolley tracks known as Germantown Avenue. Some churches are large and others are small. Day states "There are storefront churches, those smaller independent congregations in former commercial buildings; these account for almost half of the congregations in the study. Some are small, struggling to pay their bills but celebrating Jesus nonetheless. Others are solid, and informal."[15] These small churches are a staple to the lost, the disenfranchised, and without their accessibility those on the fringes of society, would have no place of formal worship or community support.

Because of the overwhelming number of small churches in urban America, they provide accessibility and a great visibility of the universal church, as they pepper the landscape like lilies in an open field. These churches are small but can be very resilient. The small church possesses a resiliency that is misunderstood and often overlooked. Their characteristics of resiliency have been foundational since the inception of the first century church.

Amanda Mantone writes "Storefront churches are lifeblood to urban poor" "In the era of the mega church, storefronts buck the trend toward massive congregations and televised PowerPoint sermons. They instead offer intimate Bible studies to which members can walk to. An urban phenomenon, storefront churches are difficult to study because so many are started by un-ordained ministers and are independent of denominational hierarchies. But they are the lifeblood in urban communities plagued by violence and economic depression, picking up where government leaves off with social services and reaching those considered beyond help."[16]

Katie Day reveals that although small congregations may reach few people, they make important contributions to urban life in at least three areas.

These areas include but are not limited to, providing food for the hungry, allowing for artistic expression, and assisting with meaningful job placements. While the size may be small, small churches have a great impact in urban communities."[17]

It is these small churches that continually proclaim the gospel message in communities that have long been forgotten. They shine the light of Jesus in the darkest of societies, presenting themselves as cities of refuge for those seeking comfort, forgiveness and healing.

There are two things that we can glean from the image of the small church as "cities of refuge" as found in Joshua 20:1-7. The first is that they were visible. In verse seven we read "So they appointed Kedesh in Galilee in the mountains of Naphatali, Shechem in the mountains of Ephraim and Kirjath Arba in the mountains of Judah." This mountain top setting of the cities of refuge gave it great visibility to anyone who was in need and in fear of their lives. All they had to do is look up and they were able to see the cities in which they could find refuge, safety and salvation (not in the saving of the soul.) Second, the city of refuge had to be accessible. In verse four we read "and when he flees to one of those cities, and stands at the entrance of the gate of the city, and declares his case in the hearing of the elders of that city, they shall take him into the city as one of them, and give him a place, that he may dwell among them. The elders were at the gate, ready and accessible to those who were trying to gain entrance. It did not matter how many people were in the city, but what stands out is that these cities were available.

Small churches across America and abroad often fulfill this role as cities of refuge because of their visibility and accessibility across the urban and global landscapes.

These small storefront and corner churches that saturate our urban landscape are definitely visible, accessible, and able to provide a covering and protection in a society where evil hungers for their lives. Mantone captures this essence hidden in the nucleus of the small church, its importance as places of refuge in urban communities. She mentions the small storefront church being *"the lifeblood."*[18]

21

Very few larger congregations and even the small congregations themselves view the life-sustaining abilities they possess within their given communities. Small churches need an internal understanding of their self-worth and importance regardless of their size.

If small churches would see the greatness of God in their smallness, one could not begin to imagine the things they could accomplish for Christ. Although small churches function differently than their larger counterparts, we can understand that the universal church is one body in Christ. Small, large, or mega, Baptist, Pentecostal, Methodist or Presbyterian, we are all different, but one in Christ. We should embrace the many diversities in functions and see the collective giftedness and strengths that God can uses in the kingdom.

Different But One

The 'Baptist Union of Great Britain Small Churches Project Report' states that "A small church is not the same thing as a scaled down larger church. There is an assumption that a church of, say, 70-100 members is a typical Baptist church and therefore a church of 30-40 members should be regarded as an emaciated version of this model. The message lurks among all sections of the Union, including within small churches themselves." [19]

This pattern of thinking can cause severe damage to the psychology of small churches. When small churches subscribe to this mindset either willing or unknowingly, it can hinder the efficacy of their ability to carry out the Great Commission, due to an inferiority complex.

Not only does it damage the mindset of small churches, but it can cause a great divide in relationships with larger churches. Because of this mindset, larger churches are often viewed unfavorably by small church ministries and are not given the honest and impartial assessment due to them.

The internal emaciated view of small churches, allows them to paint larger churches with a broad brush, subsequently discounting the large church's contribution to the *Missio* Dei." [20]

The 'Baptist Union of Great Britain, Small Churches Project Report' states "If leaders and members of small churches could genuinely feel that their church (perhaps with thirty members) has an integrity and dynamic of its own, rather than being a pale imitation of a large church, there would be an immensely liberating effect." [21] This effect will not only liberate the small church, but also give them the ability to embrace the universal church of God which includes the large and mega churches.

This emaciated view can also be external in which mega churches have no need, nor do they see value in small churches, although many of its pastors hail from such. This systemic devaluing will ultimately bring division within the universal church of Jesus Christ.

While we are one, we can still celebrate our differences and function in our God given roles, and in our perspective places in the vineyard, assisting one another, praying for each other, as both small and large churches live out the power of the gospel in their context and communities. Small churches play a very important role in God's Kingdom. When the church concentrates on increasing membership or merely numerical growth, it misses the opportunity to experience the miraculous power of how small churches are used in the Kingdom of God.

To bring about the kingdom of heaven, we see that God uses the mega, larger and smaller churches in concert. Somehow we must find a method for working as one unified body in Christ. When large and small churches work together it can alleviate feelings of insufficiency and illegitimacy.

The Struggle for Legitimacy

While small churches remain resilient they continue to struggle for legitimacy within the evangelical society. In an era of satellite television with all of its mega ministries, there is a longing of the small church to be recognized as trendsetters and a legitimate authority.

Small churches are routinely not given their rightful place as proclaimers of the gospel. Sometimes this is a result of their own feelings of "being born out of due time (1 Corinthians 15:8 NKJV)." as the Apostle Paul puts it. This denial of birth right, sometimes self-imposed, and other times imposed by others, has left many small churches feeling like orphaned children, left to fend for themselves.

This struggle has led them to behave like illegitimate children, forever attempting to gain the approval of their adoptive parents, in this case forever seeking out the approval of large church ministries, as if they have all the answers to the Kingdom of God.

Anthony G. Pappas in '*Inside the Small Church*' quotes Carl S. Dudley as saying "The small church is a different kind of social entity. To compare it to the large church or mega church is apples-to- oranges comparison. The small church was again understood to be a different but equally legitimate social form of Christ's body." [22]

Being different does not make the small church inferior." It is precisely these differences that allow the small church to perform functions and enter places that are not even imagined by larger churches. The small church is tough and built for endurance.

Small But Tough

Carl Dudley in *Effective Small Churches* states "Often financially starved, frequently without a pastor, sometimes deprived of denominational contact, or intentionally independent from outside connections, the small congregation will persevere. Many members will resist the rational proposals to "save our church" through moving, merging, yoking, or teaming. The members have faith that they can hold on "somehow." [23] In the words of one frustrated denominational executive, "Small churches are the toughest: they won't grow and they won't go away." [24] This toughness is part of the intrinsic relationship of small churches and their communities. It is the birth of these relationships between small churches and community that gives reason for their existence, the community needs the church and the church needs the community. There is a mutual dependence and acceptance of each other that forms a bond. There is a need to be present and active despite depleting resources and the absence of large numbers.

The urban storefronts and small church communities possess a culture that is unique to each individual congregation as they are faced with the challenges of embracing and cultivating the communities in which they exist. In a society where mega churches are held in high regard, smaller churches often fade into obscurity, or find themselves attempting to imitate their larger counterparts.

They often find themselves driven to duplicate programs that larger churches find easy to sustain because of their resources, trying to imitate these programs with an unsustainable budget, and minimal staff, leads to frustration and closure of many small churches.

Carl Dudley reveals a solemn truth and that is; "Although the majority of churches are small, the majority of church members belong to larger congregations.

Not everyone is attracted to small churches. They may be ubiquitous and tenacious, but they are not universally appealing." [25] There is a need for a paradigm shift in the way culture views the small church.

A Theological Paradigm Shift

Looking at the small church as the norm will mean a theological paradigm shift in the way we imagine God, in relationship with humanity. Imagine how small and minute humanity is in contrast to God, but yet God still loves us.

We are left to wrestle with our ideas on how God views the small church. This shift will further cause us to reconsider our view of how evangelicals view the small church, and how the small church internalizes its own value to society.

Carl S. Dudley in *Effective Small Churches* conveys, that we cannot assume, accepting and confirming the strength of the small church, will lead to church participation and numerical growth. Understanding this concept is a key for small churches if they are going to survive in a world were big is often thought of as better. Big as better can be seen in societal thinking and has transitioned from our restaurants and car dealerships into the church." [26] We experience daily in television and commercials, where society strives to provide for us products that are bigger and better. Subconsciously, we are driven the look for the biggest and largest in all of life's comforts, even in our worship experiences. Bigger churches, cathedrals, ministries, concerts, and the list can go on and on.

David Ray in *The Big Small Church Book* suggests, the failure to appreciate things small is at the core of problems faced by the small church. We fail to see the incredible information carrying capacity of the tiny computer chip, the herculean powers of the little ant, the incredible potential for good or bad found in the atom, our culture is enamored, and obsessed with bigness. The biggest pumpkin, hamburger, skyscraper, fish, Gross National Product, sex organs, salary, muscle and church are the measure of excellence." [27]

Let us be sure to note that there is nothing wrong with big churches; they play a very important role in God's Kingdom, and can do things that small churches dare not imagine. But we must remember to embrace the value of small churches and the gifts they offer at the Lord's table, in hopes of uniting both large and small churches to carry out the mission of God, also known as the *Missio* Dei.

This mission of God is to share the gospel in all the world as seen in (Matthew 28). This can be embraced by small and large churches alike.

The Power Beyond Resources

Larger churches do a tremendous job in allowing their resources to help them spread the gospel far beyond what the small church could dream. Creating a word and deed ministry is what makes them attractive to many people cross culturally. Larger churches are able to bring the written word into action through its resources.

They help and sustain smaller churches, but this is usually done across the continent and usually do not focus their resources locally, to assist small urban congregations. They provide the much needed medicine for health care, digging wells for fresh water in villages, providing food for the hungry, and building houses for the homeless. They are able to do wonderful works and are faithful with the resources that God has given them for the most part. On the other hand, small churches struggle with resources on a daily basis and have learned to operate out of a different paradigm, while relying on the supernatural provisions of the Lord.

One of the major problems that face small churches, are their limited resources. Limited resources can affect the ministry and outreach programs that small churches desire to engage in. Community involvement can only be stretched so far on a limited budget. Most urban small churches are planted in communities that are poor and marginalized, where the people are suffering in poverty and looking for the church to provide food programs, assistance with housing, and multi-leveled social needs. Government agencies will only provide the basic needs and often fan the flames of poverty in their governmental approach. In order to receive the help that these governmental agencies provide, one must remain in a state of poverty or the assistance will be denied or cut off. It is then that the community turns towards the small church with its limited resources, which often feels inadequate to respond to the community and its request for assistance.

Resources play a major role in what programs the small church can organize and the ministries it can effectively engage in. The limited resources can hinder the applications of single ministries, children's camps, youth outings, and an array of adult programs causing families to seek out larger churches that can provide these programs/ ministries to meet their needs. One can hardly blame people for seeking out the best venues for their children and families, especially in a world where the youth are offered much more by non-Christian agencies.

The small urban church can overcome its limited resource problem by adjusting the way it operates with what God has given it, and by redefining what God has called each individual church to do.

Anthony G. Pappas states that "while the opportunities for ministry before us are limitless, our capacity to be effective is not. Consequently, a realistic evaluation of the gifts and opportunities God has placed before the church has forced us to specialize.

When we realize that it is impossible for the church to be all things to all people, the congregations would do well by concentrating its efforts in the specific areas where God has especially equipped them." [28]

Peter Bush & Christine O'Reilly in '*Where 20 or 30 Are Gathered*' echoes this sentiment, and gives a warning to small churches that become fixated on its resources or lack thereof. They state "when leaders and members focus almost exclusively on the shortage of resources, then discouragement, fatigue, and a sense of entrapment can haunt a small church. Such an obsession reduces the desire both to worship with enthusiasm and to minister with vision." [29]

The survival of the small church depends on its ability to redirect its focus, not on a shortage of resources, but rather on the gifts that God has given to each individual small church. A celebration of these gifts and the use of them as target points for engaging community and culture will raise the self-esteem of small urban churches and the small church globally.

All churches struggle with resources, although they struggle on different levels. The larger the church, the more resources are in demand to sustain their huge auditoriums and television ministries. Conversely, the smaller the church, the less resources are in demand for sustainability. The concentration on the specific giftedness of each small church, is one of the keys to small church survival. The small church must learn to operate in its unique gifts, it is only then will the small church find strength and fulfillment from within regardless of resources.

The Choice of Bivocational

Even when small churches function in their gifted areas, and reduce spending where it can, most small churches continue to struggle with budget issues. Because of this financial strain, more and more small church pastors are choosing to function in bivocational roles. Maintaining outside employment in addition to their pastoral duties often help to relieve the congregation of budget burdens concerning pastoral salaries. Bivocational clergy is a growing movement in all smaller congregations. Transformations has taken place among mainline clergy who once felt the need for full time status, now they feel that they are called to be tentmakers."[30]

These pastors and ministers in well to do communities have sustainable congregations and have reached a plateau in membership. Some congregations have even declined, and like their urban counterparts, they have now yielded to the idea of acquiring employment outside of their daily ministerial duties.

Bivocational pastors maintain their church and secular employments. They simply add to their current responsibilities to support the church in which they serve.

This rebirth of bivocationalism, has allowed small churches to continue its function in the community, relieve salary stressors on the budgets while providing financial support to the church." [31]

Lyle E. Schaller suggests, that tentmaking is not a new concept, during the nineteenth century and part of the twentieth century, Baptist, Nazarene, Holiness, Methodist, Christian, and Presbyterian preachers gained most of their income from tentmaking." [32] It appears from Schaller's book that small church ministry was the norm for the church community, not frowned upon, nor appeared illegitimate.

Schaller also demonstrates that bivocational ministry was a cross-cultural and cross-denominational practice. Schaller conveys, that a growing number of bivocational ministers have graduated from an accredited theological seminary, have been ordained and recognized as full-time clergy in their denomination. These ministers are a key to supporting the life of small churches." [33]

In the previous chapter we reviewed some research and thinking about small church ministry. In the next chapter we will review the experience of Christ Bible Fellowship, a small church doing effective ministry. We will study them as they move from inception towards identity, growth and maturity.

Chapter Two

Small Beginnings / A Personal Ministry Experience

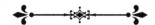

Called to Church Plant

In this chapter we will review the experience of The Christ Bible Fellowship Church as a small church doing effective ministry. We will share in their calling, the decision to obey, church planting experience, and transplant into a different urban community. The maturation of this small urban church will be revealed as they struggled with growth, church decline, limited facilities, and a decision to follow God. It is our hope that the experience of this small urban church, will help others ministries recognize and embrace their calling as a small church. This chapter will provide encouragement as it reveals the pitfalls that a small church may encounter as they join God in mission.

Jesus declared "For where two or three are gathered in my name, there am I in the midst of them" (Matthew 18:20 RSV). It is upon these words that a small church ministry was born. God called Mike and Lynne, a husband and wife to become church planters in the urban city of Philadelphia, in the state of Pennsylvania. This city is commonly called the City of Brotherly Love. It is well noted for its rich history steep on the tradition of patriotism. Philadelphia houses Independence Hall, the great Liberty Bell, and showcases such sites as the Battle of Germantown, and nearby Valley Forge.

Although steep in tradition and multiculturalism, it is also diverse, with lower, middle, and upper class residents, all sharing life in their different perspectives. Katie Day reference this diversity in *"Faith on the Avenue."*[34]

Mike and Lynne really had no idea of what it meant to plant a church in such a context, and searched for a working definition of what the phrase "church planter" would encompass.

Richard Yates Hibbert in The Place of Church Planting in Mission: Towards a Theological Framework quotes Aubrey Malphurs' definition of church planting as "a planned process of beginning and growing new local churches. Inherent in his definition are three key concepts: (1) Church planting is an intentional activity which involves human planting (2) church planting is a dynamic process; (3) church planting involves both starting new churches and helping those churches grow."[35]

While understanding church planting had to be an intentional and a well thought out process, there was also a need to trust God's sovereign will. With this strong sense of calling from God and leading of the Holy Spirit, along with much prayer and fasting, they surrendered to the will of God. The reason we use the word surrendered, is, because for a while they pushed against the idea of church planting, and resisted the call of God until it could no longer be ignored. Mike and Lynne examined many reasons of why they should not plant a church, but in the end they submitted to the call of God.

This husband and wife team were currently in a mega church in Philadelphia, enjoying wonderful experiences, while being active in the prison, men's and women's ministries. This church was home to over four thousand believers in regular attendance. It also hosted more ministries than one could ever hope for. Its worship services were vibrant, jubilant and full of life. Although being very active in this church, there was still this sense of God's calling to become church planters of a small church. First, the Holy Spirit led Mike and Lynne to scale down from a mega church to a large church.

There they continued to be active in ministry while God prepared them for roles in the small urban church. This preparation became evident in the form of the leading and teaching of small groups and home Bible studies throughout the city. They also started a drug addictions ministry in which they connected with the community, and gained a sense of what it meant to be missional and relational. This was different than the ministry in the four thousand-member church they had left. While still developing the idea of church planting, they still had no clue of what it meant to pastor a small urban congregation, but deep inside knew, that church planting had to be community focused, and relationships would be one of the keys to its success.

In February of 2003, Mike and Lynne submitted to the call of church planting within their home. With faith and obedience, they planted a seed by opening their home to the community for prayer, biblical teaching, and fellowship. The living room became a sanctuary, a space where they would engage in worship and biblical teaching.

How were they going to let others know what God had called them to do in their home? They were living in an urban environment where there were established churches with organized and robust worship centers, most within a stone's throw of their residence.

They struggled with doubt that anyone would come to worship in their home, with so many fully functioning churches available. But inside they were following the call of God to establish a church in their home. After much prayer, flyers were distributed throughout the neighborhood announcing worship on Sundays and biblical teaching on Wednesday evenings. Neighbors began to visit for those services. The services were informal, short and out of those meetings, The Christ Bible Fellowship Church, here after referred to as CBF, was born.

As inclement weather began to approach, in the winter of 2003, snow filled the streets of Philadelphia, and driving was almost impossible. Their small 3-bedroom row home was swamped with people that could not make it to their regular places of worship due to the heavy snow. Pretty soon Mike and Lynne found themselves dismantling the dining room furniture to make room for more seating, this scenario began to play out even after the inclement weather had passed. There were also people sitting on the steps that lead upstairs to sleeping quarters. God was truly moving in a special way. Not realizing it at that time, God had slowly guided them into small church ministry.

Spring time came, and by word of mouth people began to share with their friends and family members about the gathering of Christians in that home. Friends and families began to worship together there and a congregation was taking shape right before their eyes. On this tiny street, those that did not attend services often sat on their porches to hear the sermon and many commented on how it had blessed them.

Pretty soon the home became crowded and more space was needed. A board was elected and discussions began on the idea of moving out of the home to a larger place for continued worship. After a year of having church in that home, and many board meetings it was decided to relocate from the house to a larger facility in February 2004.

In February of 2004, the CBF family rented and old dentist office, and used it as a storefront church in the heart of a heavy Islamic community in the Germantown section of Philadelphia. It was there that the small church continued its growth. Focus remained on growing the congregation through preaching, teaching and worship. Believing that this would not be a permanent place of worship, and that God had a greater calling on their lives, they continued to look for a bigger facility for additional ministries.

There was still something missing, the community feeling had left them, their concentration was now on numbers, and how to grow the church. Mike and Lynne went to many seminars and training sessions such as, The Institute on Church Growth. The focus on the community had been redirected to church growth and a bigger and better building. Strategies for raising funds were developed and focused had slowly shifted. Doing things in their own strength had taken priority, it was with their power and dollars that a bigger facility would be obtained. This small urban church had not realized they had strayed from the direction in which God was leading.

Home Is Where the Church Is

In year two at the new location, CBF felt like a patient who has taken a sedative, and was drifting slowly into a relaxed and almost unconscious state. The CBF congregation drifted slowly, without realizing the direction in which they were heading. They were focused solely on buying a larger church building and counting the number of congregants. Looking forward to becoming a large church, they concentrated on numbers and not souls.

Consumed with measuring up to the larger churches and making a name for themselves, a stage to showcase the gifts of preaching, became a priority. After moving from the small church that existed in their home, Mike and Lynne thought no more of connecting to community and engaging them throughout the daily activities of life.

The thoughts were continually focused on growing numerically and raising enough money to buy a bigger building, one that would provide space for more ministry activities. The mega church ideology had eased its way into hearts unnoticed.

By 2006, the days of coming out of their home after service and sitting for hours on various porches sharing the gospel was now a thing of the past. Although pushed to the back of their minds, surely they missed that small home being the center for worship in the community, and the relationships shared with neighbors.

CBF continued in building a bigger congregation, thinking that this is what God had called them to do. Slowly being aroused, Mike and Lynne began to miss the sweet aroma of the small church ministry that was left behind in the home based church. Not having that community involvement and the intimacy of having church in the home created a desert feeling and thirst for home, truly home is where the church is. When the church moved out of their home, so did the connection with the community. They no longer engaged in spontaneous encounters with residents on the block as they traveled to and from their home. The meaningful conversations into the late night ceased. It finally occurred, that when the church moved to another location, a message was unintentionally communicated that their home was no longer the center for worship.

The Exodus into Small Church Ministry

The congregation continued its growth to about 125 members in their small storefront church, although it barely had enough room for 40. Frustration manifested as limited space in the new location in

Germantown, stifled opportunities for ministry activities. The effects of such a cramped worship space, took its toll on the congregation. Families began to leave for more vibrant and spacious places of worship. Many sought out congregations that had robust youth activities and an array of adult ministries. One could hardly blame them, as they desired to be a part of the cultural mindset of bigness.

They sought out opportunities to be part of fellowships that were good for their children, and satisfied the human desire, to belong to something big. The emptiness of their departure was deeply felt. The membership slowly decreased to 8 in attendance on any given Sunday and feelings that God had abandoned them began to permeate their thoughts. Mike and Lynne questioned their call into the church planting ministry, and longed for the days of sitting on the porch talking to neighbors about Christ.

Had the call to small church ministry been abandoned? With a drastic decline in membership hope was dissipating, and directions seemed unclear. Where was God leading? Self-examination and exploration to determine if there was something not being done correctly, yielded no fruit. Conferences on church growth were attended, and many books were read on how to grow a church, not realizing that God was still preparing this congregation for small church ministry. Continuing to pray and minister to the eight souls that God allowed to remain, CBF waited desperately to hear from the Lord.

They were now back to an intimate small church setting, but in a community where there were other worship practices. One of the most visible and active worship practices was Islam. With multiple masjids surrounding the church and their large memberships, it was difficult for CBF to engage the community with such a small congregation and Islamic vendors lining the corridor. This community was a business district by day, and a community of bars and taverns by night. Closing the church doors became a reality. Even now the focus was still centered on numbers, but deep inside Mike and Lynne longed for the days of that small urban church in their home. They remembered those meaningful conversations that occurred instantaneously while sweeping off the front porch.

The sharing of the works of the Lord while putting out the trash, and the many ways relationships were forged in that small home church community.

It was during this period in ministry a call was received to come and worship with another congregation that was on the brink of closing its doors. This church was dying in the midst of a community that was in a constant state of transition. This congregation had reached its physical maturity and found it difficult to identify with the community any longer. They had been active in ministering for well over 80 years and now lacked the strength to continue. The environment had become hostile and unfamiliar to them. De-industrialization had taken its toll as factories that once made the community vibrant left for the distant suburbs. This industrial flight de-stabilized the community as unemployment settled in. This had now become a strange environment for this congregation. Sadly, the experience was all too common as the face of American society changed and dramatically impacted the urban landscape.

Thomas J. Sugrue in *The Origins of the Urban Crisis, Race and Inequality in Postwar Detroit* conveys the sentiment of: Urban deindustrialization and the disinvestment along with White flight into suburbanization, were some of the causes that created the poor urban environments that exists today. One of the greatest migrations of the twentieth century was the movements of Whites from central cities to the suburbs. The suburban bureaucracy used their money and power to enforce zoning laws, that ultimately labeled and denied, those in the low and middle income brackets as outsiders. The people most affected by this were people of color."[36]

This strategy of denying funding and the movement of industrial plants and factories from the urban communities to White suburbia, greatly affected the living conditions of urban neighborhoods. It also provoked hopelessness and despair while providing a breeding ground for uncontrolled anger within these communities across the globe. The community that we had been invited to, faced these same issues, as they struggle to survive in these conditions.

Dr. Ron Daniels president of the Institute of the Black World echoes this sentiment in Reasserting the Vision/Mission of Black Nationalism: Deindustrialization raided the urban communities of the low and semi-skilled jobs. These jobs afforded African Americans with limited education a chance to work for decent wages. The wages provided for the household and sustained the Black family. The resolution to disinvest, and remove jobs that the Black family needed to survive, were made by forces exterior to Black communities. After these decisions were made, work for the Black male was almost non-existent. The federal government failed to respond through reconstruction and investment in the Black communities. The urban community answered in a way that has changed its scenery for years."[37]

While it is not fair to say that disinvestment is responsible for all of urban life's deterioration, but it can be attributed to much of the violence that plagues our urban environments throughout major cities. Because of disinvestment, parents now had to find work farther from home, traveling greater distances for jobs. This travel often times rendered them unavailable in the home to rear children, leaving the children to fend for themselves.

It is important to note at this juncture, that small urban churches do not have a monopoly on suffering. We can find small churches in rural America suffering like their urban counterparts. The problems that plague small urban churches are similar to those that devastate small rural churches in Iowa, Minnesota, Idaho, Kansas, Nebraska just to name a few. The names and faces may change but the burden of the small church to respond is the same."[38] Deindustrialization and disinvestment in any community whether urban or rural produces the same results of despair, homelessness, suicide, hopelessness and the like. Small churches around the world are still task with the responsibility to respond to such crisis.

After several joint worship services, with the small congregation who invited us to worship, it was expressed that the Lord had directed this dwindling congregation to gift CBF the building they were worshipping in, and they encouraged CBF to come and continue to build the Kingdom of God. This came as a total shock and surprise that someone would just give away a fully functioning place of worship for free!

Although praising God for this wonderful gift on the outside, the leadership at CBF was still unsure of what God was doing. This wonderful and gracious congregation handed over the keys and deed to the church building and departed leaving CBF to ponder the marvelous works of the Lord. It was a truly amazing gift, but with only 8 members there was no way of maintaining the costs of operating such a huge facility. What were they going to do with such a large church building and a small congregation?

Large Building /Small Congregation

The church was located in an urban environment, in the Kensington section of Philadelphia. The building was old, but in great shape with little work needed in the way of repairs. It was in operating condition and fully equipped, seating about 250 comfortably and housed a huge multi-purpose room that could be used for several ministry activities. There were also 5 classrooms for instruction and learning activities. This is the kind of building Mike and Lynne had envisioned. Excited about the new facility, there was still a burning question in their hearts, why God would allow families to leave the congregation, then give such a gift? Whatever the reasons were, they were truly grateful for the new worship space.

The East Kensington section of Philadelphia was the mission field where God had caused CBF to relocate, settle, and yield to the will of God. East Kensington is surrounded by urban blight and decay from every side. Many houses are abandoned and used by those that are addicted to drugs as a place to indulge. Trash often litters the streets, which gives the community a landscape view of a war torn nation. Open drug markets are visible and operate twenty-four hours a day in what seems like a state of impunity. Alcohol and drug use is commonplace and has become the norm for this community. Prostitution is wantonly practiced and used as a tool or source for economic gain to either fuel drug and alcohol habits or to feed one's family." [39]

Most families are fatherless and grandmothers are raising grandchildren due to the absence of either one or both parents. Housing is unstable, while economic injustice in some government policies help fuel the instability.

John M. Perkins in, *Beyond Charity: The Call to Christian Community Development*, labeled the (AFDC) Aid to Families with Dependent Children as one of the most destructive agencies for the Black community. This agency failed to acknowledge the family, and did not include resources that would encourage the rebuilding of the family. Its goal was to subsidize the mother while excluding the father. This agency denied the extended family the opportunity to become part of the assistance. There was also no incentive to remove oneself from the system."[40] These and other governmental polices included, maintaining a salary wage that is at the poverty level in order to receive assistance. Policies further enforced the father's removal from the home in order to receive assistance.

Housing is usually provided by private landlords who have the ability to stop renting at any given time disrupting the stability of the family. Most landlords provide minimum maintenance of their properties forcing families to flee horrid living conditions, only to find themselves in the same situation. This situation is one of the reasons families move from house to house changing neighborhoods as many as 3-5 times in a year. The outcome of these polices design a life and an income level that is suited for poverty. Families must adhere to these polices in order to receive the non- sufficient support and food supplies provided by government agencies. Truly this community was suffering at the hands of economic injustice.

If the CBF congregation was going to make an impact in this community, they would need to respond to the reality of economic injustice. Some may ask the question what is economic injustice? To answer that question let us first look at the term economic justice.

When exploring economic justice from a biblical perspective, it is necessary to frame out a working definition. For the purpose of this study we will view economic justice from the social and spiritual perspectives. The first perspective we examine will be social.

Rolf A. Jacobson describes economic justice as a social concept. One that encompasses how society responds to humanity. This response ultimately effects the conditions in a given segment of society. This is readily seen in urban communities where the larger societal order has not responded favorably to its needs" [41]

Loosening the restrictions of government policies would allow those suffering in urban and rural communities to thrive in a social order that promotes the ideals of our founding fathers, life, liberty and the pursuit of happiness. The Bible gives a clear view of God's justice as it relates to the Israelites after they were delivered out of bondage in Egypt. God is concerned about justice not only *from without* (Pharaoh) but also *from within* the nation of Israel herself. As we look at (Exodus 23:1-13) it gives us some detailed information concerning the commandments given by God to ensure economic and social justice for all of Israel. These commandments have a social component to them not just for the nation of Israel, but also for the foreigner (slave). God has a definite concern for all of humanity regardless of the class. It is amazing to see also in this passage that God is concerned about justice for the animals as well! What a wonderful God we serve!

This leads us to the second perspective, which is spiritual. Viewing economic justice purely as social concept, can produce a distorted view of a Holy and Righteous God. Furthermore, it will not give "christotelic" intimacy (the view that all things culminate in Jesus Christ) to the biblical narrative that is deserved."[42]

Without the spiritual view, it can pave the way for such ideologies as caste systems, classism, and give credence to racism and wars. With just the idea of social justice, someone could possibly think that certain lifestyles or measures of wealth is good for a certain group or class of people. Or that certain groups are superior or inferior. Spiritual and social justice combined can show that God is concerned with our material welfare as much as our spiritual welfare. Spiritual and social justice are interdependent and symbiotic, therefore economic justice, social justice, and worship of the true and Living God must be married together in order for society to experience true justice.

Stephen Mott and Ronald J. Slider in "Economic Justice: a biblical paradigm conveys: The biblical narrative is the extensive account of God's interaction with the world. It expands from creation, through the fall and redemption of humanity, to the return of Christ. The biblical narrative gives us an awareness of the nature of the material world, and personalities of the people that dwell in it. Since every person is created to house the image of God in community, material abundance alone, will never completely satisfy the human soul. Economic life must be ordered in a way that allows for all of humanity to live a life of dignity given by the Creator. This dignity allows for the harmonious living and worship of the human race. When this dignity is eradicated through economic injustice, the image of God becomes distorted. And life as we know it is out of sync with the biblical narrative."[43]

Economic justice not only encompasses the social, but true economic justice cannot be obtained without its spiritual aspect being nurtured. "We are made for community." Mott and Slider states; when that unity is broken through deprivation of basic human needs, then the God given character and dignity which are the fabrics of life are eroded." [44]

CBF found themselves with the facility of their dreams, but in a community where economic injustice has debilitated and given birth to unprecedented levels of violence. Hope has dissipated and an ideology that God has abandoned this community has become personal testimonies of some. As a congregation that was guided to this community by the Holy Spirit, there were still burning questions: where is God in this community? What could this small church possibly accomplish in the urban environment and with so little resources? These questions and others would continue to haunt the congregation as they sought to find identity and purpose of being a small urban church in a big building and in a strange community.

The Gospel of Prosperity is prevalent in our church communities today, which could be one of the reasons larger churches continue to increase their size, and small churches continue to struggle. Most Americans want to live, connect and worship where there is prosperity. However, we will discuss more in Chapter Four, that God does not abandon us in difficult situations. Instead God is with us in those environments and invites us to join Him.

Trying to determine the core objectives for ministry in this context, would prove to be more difficult than expected. This congregation of eight canvassed the community in order to ascertain what were the needs of the people, by going from door to door talking with residents about life in the community.

One of the first things they discovered were, that people needed food, so CBF provided a food cupboard to those that were in need of food to feed their families.

Realizing the community was populated with plenty of children, free school supplies were handed out at the start of the school year, all in an effort to meet the needs of the community and to evangelize those that were lost. As resources began to diminish, it placed a strain on a congregation that was already struggling with finances. CBF fell into the trap that small urban ministries often to fall into, trying to do ministry the large church way. There were plenty of books that were written on how to reach a community and some of them were helpful, but ultimately the small urban congregation was modeling what some might call people pleasers.

Addressing the physical needs of the urban community, without giving concern to the spiritual condition is not what God intended for CBF to do. It paved the way for dependence on the church, while independent of a relationship with God. Frustration set in and tensions mounted as the community residents failed to respond in a way that increased church attendance.

The community residents desired only the material help (clothes, food, school supplies) based on the previous church's actions of meeting material needs only. The leadership team confused and bewildered, as to how to connect to the community, they turned to prayer, asking God to show the way in which to go.

The leadership fell back on its missional training as they began to teach the concept of missional theology and how it had to be central in determining their core values, as well as their mission.

CBF discovered there were different ways to do God's mission, once they found out God was present. The God of the universe was truly on a mission and they were determined to find out what it was. They asked questions such as: was God present in this community? Had God forgotten about these people? Why would God send us here and give us this building? Are there any signs of God being present and active there? These and other questions lead to long discussions and intense periods of prayer as they sought out the mission of God.

Seeking out God's mission in the study of such passages as (Luke 4:18-19), where the mission of Jesus was examined in great detail.

Here Jesus declares the mission from the Father as, "to preach the gospel, heal the broken, set captives free." (John 20:20-23), shows in the same way that Jesus was sent on mission from God, he now sends the disciples, saying "In the same way the Father has sent me I also send you (NKJV)."

In (Matthew 28:19-20), we find Jesus commissioning the disciples and sends them on mission into the world to do the Fathers will. These passages and others like them, were studied in hopes to discover the mission of God through Jesus Christ, that CBF might find its own identity and mission in Christ's mission. Examining the mission of Christ continually led back to the mission of God, which resulted in a burning question. What was God doing with this small congregation in this big building, and what is God doing in this community?

A longing to experience the presence of God in community, CBF began to focus on seeking out that presence, through the activity of the Holy Spirit. Seeking the presence of God, and not increased membership, allowed for conversations with the community during prayer walks.

Involvement in community activities became part of congregational life while seeking nothing more than the presence of God. It was through these conversations and intense listening periods the words of hope were heard. Stories of hope, views of God, and the blessings received from the Father shared. It was revealed through these times of prayer and sharing that there was a baseline belief system of an All-Sufficient and All-Powerful God in this community.

Like children waiting to unwrap their Christmas presents, excitement caught hold of the CBF congregation. They knew that wherever hope was, the presence of God was there also, because it is God who gives us hope. Searching for spiritual signs and movements revealed that God had not abandoned this community and this small church was to play a role in God's activity there. The love of Christ was very present and active in this urban environment. The understanding was forming through missional teaching and praying that Christ had invited this small urban church to yield to such activity and become an instrument in the hands of the Holy God. CBF came to understand that if they were going to be effective in mission, core values had to be aligned were God was active. Learning to see God and not numbers was not an easy task. It caused much anguish and brought about conflict within the congregation.

The Conflict

The CBF congregation read such books as *The Missional Leader by Allen J. Roxburgh and Fred Romanuk*, and realized not only was God at work in the community, but to yield to Christ they needed to experience an unleashing of spirituality within the congregation. This brought about much internal conflict. The congregation had been composed of mainly new believers, who were not yet developed in their spirituality. Attempting to yield to the activity of Christ's mission with a congregation of spiritually immature believers, presented a conflict because of their unwillingness to surrender to the will of God. Joining Christ's mission would need to be the task of mature believers, this would happen through spiritual formations. Now that the veil was lifted, CBF understood that Christ had chosen this small church with little resources and training to yield to God's mission in this community.

Allen J. Roxburgh and Fred Roman in *"The Missional Leader"* writes "If the Spirit has been poured out in the church- the church as it is, not some ideal type- then we are compelled to believe that the Spirit of God is at work and alive among the congregations of America. Congregations matter, but they need leaders with the skills to cultivate an environment in which the Spirit-given presence of God's future may emerge among the people of God." [45]

The leaders at CBF had to understand that no matter how small the congregation was, they still mattered in the mission of God, and Christ was calling them to yield in that mission. Embracing the truth that they were important to Christ's work, despite limited finances and resources, the spirit of Christ needed to be unleashed among the congregation. Somehow the congregation must internalize that they mattered to God. How could they share a love they had not yet fully embraced? The leadership had to somehow resolve this inner conflict that believed a small church was not important to God.

Daniel P. Smith and Mary K. Sellon in *"Pathways to Renewal"* writes "The church- growth movement is often blamed for leading congregations down the path of thinking that bigger is better and that increased numbers equal health and growth."[46]

While Smith and Sellon do not place all the blame on the church growth movement, they do, however, recognize that it opens our eyes to examine how we measure congregational health.

Spiritual renewal had to become the goal at CBF, not increased membership. The leadership team took a survey within the congregation by asking various questions to get an understanding of how the church was being measured, it revealed answers that were not expected. The measurements of success or failures were not by the word of God but by standards of what other churches (large churches) were doing. The hurtful part is, the leadership embraced this same measurement. In order for spiritual renewal to take place the leadership team first had to embrace that there is no ideal church model (other churches).

Christ operates differently in different types of environment. The activity of God will look different in the house church than the coffee shop church, different in the small church than the large church, different in the urban church than the rural church. CBF needed to understand God's activity in this community might differ than what others experienced in theirs. Shaking the Gideon complex found in (Judges 6:15-27), where God cause Gideon to understand that victory was assured through God's power alone, allowed for realization that there is a uniqueness in the small church and God's ability. CBF became committed not to limit what could be done through the power of God in Jesus Christ, regardless of church membership size. Instead they focused on the gifts and abilities that a small church has to offer.

Yielding to the mission and activity of Christ, called for the congregation to move towards spiritual formation. A firm understanding of just what spiritual renewal encompassed needed to be mapped out. In the next chapter we will begin to map out what renewal and spiritual formation might look like.

Chapter Three

The Need for Spiritual Formation

In this chapter, we will review the process by which the CBF congregation is transformed. Yielding to the power of the Holy Spirit, enabled the CBF congregation to experience renewal /transformation and restoration. We will examine the meaning of spiritual transformation and congregational renewal and the methods the small urban congregation used in the process. If the small church is going to be effective in Christ's mission, a true renewal and transformation must take place within the church. This renewal/transformation will allow the church to see themselves through the eyes of God, while challenging its motives and behavioral practices. It is my desire that readers experience this process along with CBF as this chapter is explored.

If CBF was going to experience renewal and see spirituality unleashed within the congregation, they needed a working definition of what this might look like. Sellon and Smith *in Pathways to Renewal Practical Steps for Congregations* contends:

Congregational renewal is the capacity of humanity to be aware of, and experience the presence of God in their daily lives. Congregational renewal creates a longing to join God in carrying out salvation plans for the world. The end result of renewal is an understanding of the relationship between God and humanity. Renewal forges a relationship of understanding between church, community and calling."[47]

This definition thoroughly described the state of CBF and resonated with how they were feeling about their relationship with God and community. This realization would be one of the keys to unlock the door to spiritual renewal within the congregation. Spiritual renewal would give them identity, purpose and direction. Before they could help others see Jesus, the congregation must first experience the fullness, of the love of Christ in their own lives. This *agape* love is not measured by buildings or membership size, but rather upon the gracious love of the Father sending the Son, to shed the precious blood of Christ for all of humanity. This included the small church.

Understanding this dynamic was the catalyst to freedom that the leadership team so desperately needed. Experiencing God in their midst helped to conceptualize that spiritual renewal was not something that could be done through programs, and outreach, nor through church growth seminars. It was truly the work of the Holy Spirit in each member individually and the church body. The task now set before the leadership was to teach and cultivate an understanding of what a God centered relationship might look like. Embracing this understanding would provide the fallow ground needed for the Holy Spirit to demonstrate power, according to the Spirit's will, through yielded hearts and spirits.

A yielded heart and spirit would be the home where the Holy Spirit of God could rest. The things that CBF were doing were not totally wrong, but without the Spirit's leading and directing, they were empty of spiritual significance. Their actions were based on human efforts. Programs to feed the hungry were biblical mandates and practices, clothing the naked was a command of Christ Jesus (Matthew 25:42-43.) The giving out school supplies relieved parents of burdens, but none of these produced spiritual renewal. These were deeds done apart from any real love for the receivers. CBF had to be sure, that it actions were born out of love for God, and God's people, and not just deeds.

When a church becomes deed-oriented, they fail to desire the things that God desires such as, repentant hearts. This can become an obstacle blocking the view of Christ.

With a newfound understanding, CBF had to be very careful not to create a sense of urgency that John P. Kotter writes about in

Leading Change: "Whether taking a firm that is on its knees and restoring it to health, making an average contender the industry leader, establishing a sense of urgency is crucial to gaining needed co-operation."[48]

A sense of urgency would drive CBF to practices designed for the business world, and not suited for the work of the Holy Spirit. The process of renewal and restoration had to be worked out in the timing of the one who is actually doing the renewal. Renewal is the work of the Holy Spirit and not the leadership team. The temptation to become work-oriented again, would place the congregation on its own timetable, blinding it from the activity of God. To create a sense of urgency would also create a standard of measurement that would not be sensitive to spiritual renewal. This process of spiritual renewal could not be rushed to results, but rather patiently yielding to the Holy Spirit as renewal is created in hearts and minds as disciples of Christ.

Walking slowly and allowing the Holy Spirit the freedom to move, while keeping the faith, allowed for renewal to take place. As hearts and minds were being renewed, the need for spiritual disciplines surfaced. These disciplines would transform the congregation from the inside moving outward.

Spiritual disciplines had to be worked out in detail. The disciplines could not be rushed, allowing the Holy Spirit to permeate minds, bodies, and souls.

This required prayer and fasting. Where do we go from here? This was the question that CBF began to ask the Holy Spirit. Where did he want to rest in our lives? Through much praying and fasting CBF was lead of the Spirit to spend time in learning what it meant to be a disciple.

Going back to the foundational work of Jesus Christ dying for humanity, and commissioning the Twelve was a key. The focus had shifted from getting the community to participate in worship, to God preparing the church as a vessel to receive such a gift as this community. After three years, realization set in that CBF was called to be something, other than acting as church goers, and that something was to be Christ's disciples. They were called to be Christ's disciples regardless of their size. What a wonderful realization!

The Spiritual Formation of Discipleship

Juan Carlos Ortiz in *Called to Discipleship* writes "One of the most controversial and misunderstood teachings of the Bible is how to make disciples. I'm always hesitant when asked to explain this concept, because it can be construed as mechanics. People can be tempted to copy it. And if you put this thing into practice without the renewal of the whole congregation you are going to become frustrated."[49] CBF had experienced this frustration before, and understood very well that mechanical Christianity devoid of the Spirit of God is unfruitful.

Congregational Renewal was the gateway for discipleship formation to take place within the congregation. It was necessary to establish a foundation that would cultivate this discipline. Based on Matthew 28 and the command to make disciples, CBF began to flesh out what that command entailed.

If discipleship was the goal, then the church needed to get a full understanding of what discipleship actually meant. Once again, we came together for prayer and fasting asking the Holy Spirit for revelation on what biblical discipleship would look like in this congregation.

A congregational study of Dietrich Bonhoeffer's book *The Cost of Discipleship,* would be one of the tools used. Bonhoeffer's book was suggested to the CBF leadership team, during a discipleship training session. It also agreed with Pastor Mike's reformed theology training. It was would be very instrumental in helping the congregation understand just what it meant to be a disciple of Jesus Christ, by understanding the means of grace.

Bonhoeffer first deals with grace, in that grace is not cheap. He defines cheap grace as "Justification of sin without justification of the sinner."[50] Now if this is true, then true discipleship can never take place within a believer's life without one realizing the cost of what is required for the sinner to be justified. Reading Bonhoeffer's book encouraged the congregation to embrace the value and importance of the cost of grace. Yes, grace is free, but it is not cheap. He goes on to further describe cheap grace as "The preaching of forgiveness without requiring repentance, baptism without church discipline,

Communion without confession, absolution without personal confession. Cheap grace, is grace without discipleship, grace without the cross, grace without Jesus Christ, living and incarnate."[51]

What a concept! CBF had never connected grace and discipleship together before. Grace to CBF had been thought of as something that happened at the cross and seen in incidents throughout life.

Grace had been relegated to the saving from a car accident, a good report from the doctor, the receiving of steady employment. Although these events may be the results of grace, grace is much deeper than this.

Discipleship is the stage where grace is showcased and applauded as a gift from the Father. Grace can be viewed as that gift from God through Christ, that calls and even demands commitment and obedience to the will of God. Bonhoeffer says "The first step, to discipleship, which follows the call, cuts the disciple off from his previous existence. The call to follow at once produces a new situation. To stay in the old situation makes discipleship impossible."[52] Bonhoeffer's book became the Sunday school study for a year. Through open discussions and preaching moments, steps were put into action on how to cut off the old situation, and walk in the new calling of the Spirit. The study of such passages as Ephesians 4:17-32 and Colossians 3:1-17 yielded biblical support and encouragement. Out of these studies questions arose, such as how do we cut off the "old man"? And how is renewal cultivated in the "new man"?

Bonhoeffer lends the idea; the call to follow Christ, beckons us to form an exclusive connection to the person of Christ. This connection is a form of grace that breaks the bonds of self-righteousness. This call transcends the law, and calls the disciple through grace to a life of obedience. Discipleship then means to devote oneself totally to Christ as the sole object of affection, carried out in mind, body and soul. Discipleship calls for total submission to the person of Christ and God's redeeming grace."[53] Studying Bonhoeffer gave CBF the opportunity to flesh out the command to follow Jesus and weigh the commitment that ensued. Small spurts of growth were emerging as changed behaviors and spiritual formation surfaced."[54]

There were times of congregational struggle to revert back to the "old man" or as Bonhoeffer puts it "the old situation."[55] Unfortunately, some members could not surrender to spiritual formation and they left the congregation. The leadership connected with other pastors and ministers in the city, that were active in discipleship trainings. These leaders also viewed discipleship as a way to unleash spirituality within congregations.

Through much prayer and leading of the Spirit, CBF connected with City Net Ministries in Philadelphia through Dr. Edward Gross, author of, *Are You a Christian or a Disciple?* Gross challenges the 21st century disciple, with biblical discipleship. He compares the disciples that followed Jesus to 21st century disciples, in order to discover true discipleship. Gross is an international speaker and trainer in discipleship models around the world. He presently trains churches of any size in how to become and make disciples. Gross writes "there is no biblical Christianity apart from biblical discipleship. Acts 11 proclaims that the disciples were called Christians.... They were disciples before they were called Christians. If you want to follow Christ, He is always available. But not on your terms."[56] It is through his book and disciple-making trainings the church was challenged on its view and commitment to biblical discipleship. CBF was challenged to examine themselves individually and collectively around the terms of their discipleship. Was it on Christ's terms? Congregational terms? Personal terms? Gross writes "Today we have Christianity without the living Christ as its authority figure. In His place we have set up a calm and benign Christ who does not demand too much. A quiet coupe has occurred and Jesus has been chased away."[57]

This book study and teaching on discipleship allowed the congregation to focus on their relationship with Jesus Christ and not numerical growth of a congregation.

Juan Carlos Ortiz echoes this sentiment in *Disciple: A Handbook for New Believers*. He demonstrates through the Scriptures that following Jesus must be done on Christ's terms and not ours. He writes how the rich young ruler in (Luke 18:18) had done all that he knew to do as required by the law, but could not imagine parting with his possessions. Unless the rich young ruler was willing to part with everything including his possessions, he could not fully and truly follow Jesus. For to follow Jesus means that nothing can come between

Christ and the follower. It is impossible for a disciple to follow Christ on his or her own terms."[58]

Cultivating spiritual formation in the area of discipleship was crucial to the congregation. If true renewal and formation were to occur, CBF would have to be committed to follow Jesus as Lord and on Christ's terms, not theirs. Much discussion was given as to what it looks like to follow on Jesus terms, and what life looks like when the congregation operates on its terms. Passages that Juan Ortiz used in his book, such as Luke 19:10, where he writes about Zacchaeus submitting to the Lordship of Jesus were examined. In Luke 9:59, where Jesus commanded another man to follow him above all, even before the burial of his father. These and similar passages provided a spring board for discussions and personal inventory of how these applied as a church body.

Jon Coe in Resisting the Temptation of Moral Formation: Opening To Spiritual Formation In The Cross And The Spirit contends, "... Some Christians approach discipleship much like a shopper leisurely browse the stores in a mall.

Frequently stopping to admire and purchase the things that appeal to their intellect and emotions. This kind of approach to discipleship lacks a serious adherence to a life of obedience. With this kind of discipleship one will find it difficult to experience the Spirit's transformation. A disciple that is void of an obedient life, leaves the door open to misuse the grace of God, rendering the Lord's work on the cross to temporal blessings and protection from eternal punishment."[59]

Coe writings on moral formation lends to the idea that humanity inherently yearns for some type of formation even if it is moral, in search of the spiritual. Coe makes a compelling argument for moral formation versus spiritual transformation. However other people may believe that there is much room for speculation of why these behaviors and thought patterns exists. One might raise the question: Could moral formation be the result of misguided doctrines of what biblical discipleship should model?

With countless churches: mega, large, small, local, global, and all with various denominations, a buffet of discipleship models has been offered. This buffet includes (ancient, contemporary, intellectual, moral, safe, inward, and outward) formations of discipleship.

Some have been provided by well-intentioned leadership. For some, moral formation has been cultivated out of culture, family values, and societal practices.

Discipleship models that are void of total submission (mind, body and spirit) to the will of Christ, creates tension between the flesh and the spirit. Paul writes in Galatians 5:17 "For the flesh wars against the Spirit and the Spirit against the flesh." It is this battle that disciples wrestle with daily. Essentially, discipleship in Christ Jesus is a call to total spiritual transformation through obedience and submission.

Dallas Willard writes in "Spiritual Formation And The Warfare Between The flesh And The Human Spirit": "Spiritual formation in Christ is the process through which disciples or apprentices of Jesus take on the qualities or characteristics of Christ himself, in every essential dimension of human personality. The overall orientation of their will, the kinds of thoughts and feelings that occupy them, the automatic inclinations and readiness of their body inaction, the prevailing posture of their relations toward others, all through the formative processes undergone by his disciples, increasingly come to resemble the personal dimensions of their Master."[60]

This type of spiritual formation embodies the will, thoughts, feelings, and actions, it manifests itself in love. When biblical discipleship formation is lived out in all of life, it identifies itself in love sent down from the Father. For the true mark of a disciple of Jesus Christ is that of love. In (John 13:35 NKJV) Jesus declares "By this all will know you are my disciples, if you have love for one another." A Christ- like love, is the defining mark of a disciple, of the Master. Therefore, CBF would do well to cultivate this love from within, to enable sharing in the community. Although they did love one another, the question is, were they loving each other as directed by Christ? Were they exemplifying the love of the 1st century disciples? Was the modeling of biblical discipleship authentic, and rooted in Christ's love?

The Spiritual Formation of Love

How could CBF be sure what congregational love looked like from the inside out? Continuing in prayer, asking God to speak through the biblical text, they wrestled with how to cultivate love for one another. Just how was this mark of love made visible within the congregation?

In (John 13:34-35) Jesus states, "A new commandment I give to you, that you love one another; as I have loved you, that you also love one another.

By this all will know that you are My disciples, if you have love for one another." Spiritual formation without the qualifying mark of biblical love, is not really spiritual formation at all. This study of Jesus' words in the book of John was impressed upon the hearts of CBF that love for one another must be at the core of discipleship. The leadership and congregation examined multiple passages that spoke of love, in order to grasp this love that defined us as disciples of Jesus Christ.

Walvoord & Zuck in The Bible Knowledge Commentary suggest on (John 13:34-35) The survival of the disciples depended upon their ability to obey the command of Jesus to love one another. The disciples were used to a common love, practice by humanity, but the love that Jesus instructed was powered by the Holy Spirit. This kind of love is based on the blood atoning love of Christ. The disciples love was to strengthen, encourage and support one another in trails as they preached to gospel to those who received it and those who rejected it. Not only did this love promote strength and unity, but it also allowed the world to see Jesus."[61]

Without this sacrificial love as the root of every believer, Christians in the 21st century would run the risk of fracturing the body of Christ through independent worship practices. While independent Christianity seems harmless it does not model the intent of Jesus for the disciples. Stephen Hong uses the terminology of "Hyper Individualism," in his article Reversing A Downward Spiral: Strengthening The Church's Community, Holiness And Unity Through Intentional Discipleship: He suggests that too many Christians view their faith as a private matter. Something that is between them and God only, excluding the larger congregation.

This he suggests can even happen in the communal worship experience. Although believers are worshipping together, they are not connected to one another." [62] Hong's assessment of "hyper individualism" in the 21ˢᵗ century Church, can often be heard throughout congregations in the urban African American church communities. This trend of individualism hardens the ground, and creates a difficult environment for the spiritual formation of love, to take root. Galatian (6:2) admonishes us to "Bear one another's burdens and so fulfill the law of Christ."

This bearing of burdens is done through love, that disciples of the Master have for one another. It allows for the sharing of the triumphs and pitfalls of the Christian community and serves as a life line in turbulent waters.

Glenn Daman writes in *Shepherding the Small Church* "the idea that a Christian would want to (or even could) live independently of the rest of the community was completely foreign and smacked of failure to understand and appropriate the love and sanctifying work of Christ. John said it most forcefully when he wrote that the failure to love the brother was a mark of carnality and of being unregenerate (1 John 3:14)."[63]

CBF needed an intentional dismantling of individualism, and a concentrated effort of oneness, in communal worship and life together. This intentionality would help to foster obedience to the command of sacrificial love towards one another given by Jesus.

Simon Schrock writes in *One Anothering* "Renewal begins when we acknowledge that our hearts are not full of love, that they are, in fact, empty. Renewal comes when our confession brings us to God crying for mercy- and the grace to love as we ought."[64]

Schrock reminds us of practical ways to love and encourage one another. He urges us to seek out the welfare and interest of each other in communal life and list such ways as: (cheer up your team, urge the other upward, divinely love one another, stepping toward heavenly fellowship, consume not one another, just to name a few).

Using Schrock's book as a spring board for acts of one anothering, CBF, began creating tangible opportunities to cultivate love within the congregation. Having a small church congregation would lend itself to the goal. Leadership brainstorming, led to ideas that would create a flow of one anothering through fellowships. Once a month house-to-house fellowships, of those who would use their homes for hospitality, created opportunities for anyone who wanted to come for food, fellowship and games. It was during this time, bonds formed as they laughed together, ate together, and practice love for one another outside the communal worship experience of Sunday morning. The intimacy of fellowship in homes, with the children included, led to discovering genuine concerns of each other. Job information and assistance was given, clothing items shared, needs were verbalized. This spiritual formation of love flowed into the Sunday morning worship experience. True communal worship could now be experienced.

At these home fellowships, disciples shared with each other the burdens that had afflicted them, and praying for each other became common sight. The home fellowship gave birth to an informal annual first Sunday's dinner in the church. After communion worship service, everyone who was willing, brought a dish, and a common meal would be shared. This provided an open door for Sunday morning visitors to experience this discipleship of love. As visitors began to participate in these fellowships, a glimpse of God's leading was internalized.

On one worship occasion, offering was collected, hymns sung, then everyone piled into cars. A small caravan was then led on an hour's drive to the beach for a sermon by the ocean, fellowship, food and fun! This act caused congregants to ride with others that they may not have associated with outside the worship setting. It was in these cramped car rides to the shore that love and sharing was expressed throughout.

There was one instance when one of the children of the church was rushed to the emergency room due to a sudden illness. Being a small congregation they were able to close Bible study at the church and move it to the emergency waiting room. While in the waiting room members prayed and waited for God's healing hand. Others in the waiting area experienced their love for one another, and began to inquire about the location of the church. Learning to love one another sacrificially like Christ, created a unity within.

That unity enabled sharing in a way that resembled the 1st century disciples in Acts 2. Loving the way that Christ commands us, is a spiritual matter. Although this love is manifested in acts of the flesh, its root is spiritual. Because this love is spiritually rooted, there is also a spiritual enemy that opposes this Christ centered love.

Paul writes in (Romans 7:21 AMP) "So I find it to be a law (rule of action of my being) that when I want to do what is right and good, evil is ever present with me and I am subject to its insistent demands."

Sin is an ever present obstacle to the believer's spiritual formation. True spiritual formation cannot take place unless sin in the disciple's life is addressed and confessed daily. Without the daily confession of sin, there remains and opportunity to grieve the Holy Spirit and hinder the work of spiritual formation within the believer. Next we will examine sin as an obstacle to spiritual formation.

Spiritual Formation and Sin

CBF had to change its thinking, from membership to discipleship, through spiritual renewal, with love as the core. This love must guard against sin that seeks to destroy it. An understanding of the nature of sin would be a priority in CBF's spiritual renewal and formations.

Peter Nelson in Discipleship Dissonance: Towards A Theology of Imperfection Amidst the Pursuit of Holiness conveys: The disciple often finds him or herself torn once they are aware of what holiness is, as they attempt to practice it in their daily lives. This happens when we view holiness as a target of pureness or a goal to achieved, instead of a consistent way of living in community. Biblical writers acknowledge this tension as they encourage their readers to pursue holiness. 1 John 1:9 helps us to relive this tension with instructions to confess our sins that we may receive forgiveness as we follow Jesus."[65]

The view that Nelson gives is liberating and encouraging. Nelson's view allows for a fallen humanity to get back up with the determination to follow Christ and continue to pursue holiness. This is not to advocate that sin should be viewed lightly or half-heartedly, but even when humanity falls into sin, a proper view will allow for liberation to take place. Liberation through failure happens when the disciple of Christ understands sin in the lives of believers, as they follow Jesus.

57

Sin in the believer's life often hinders spiritual formation. An improper view of sin can derail a disciple and stunt his or her spiritual growth. For instance, a disciple of Jesus Christ who views sin improperly, may contend that they are able to follow Christ living a life of intentional and unconfessed sin. Another problem that the believer faces, is when sin is viewed through the lenses of perfection.

If the believer does not achieve that perfection in their Christian walk, a succumbing to it can devastate their faith. This failure to reach the perfection of sinlessness, can be the reason some quit trying to live a holy life, and walk away from the faith. Instead they need to understand that not living a life style of sin is the journey and not the goal on this side of heaven. (1John 1:9 NKJV) says "If we confess our sins."

The Bible is clear that in our humanity we will occasionally sin. We should not submit to such, but seek to journey without committing such acts. However, when we do, we must realize that there is grace, forgiveness and the blood of Christ that cleanses us.

After much prayer and fasting, it was decided that James would be the book of study as it details sin and the results thereof in the believer's life. James details sin and its direct origins, behaviors, and growth. The book of James models how the believer should respond to his or her person, desires and motives as it relates to sin. PowerPoint presentations and sermons would be the method that CBF chose to educate the congregation on sin.

If understanding the dynamics of sin and its consequences were not fully brought to the surface, then spiritual formation would be hindered. The doctrine of sin must be brought to the surface, for spiritual formation to be effective. Sin was truly an obstacle to the renewal of CBF, and ultimately can prevent total yielding to the Holy Spirit. A series of sermons on the "Deceitfulness of Sin" were developed from the book of James. These sermons and teaching took form in the following manner.

The Deceitfulness of Sin

A source of blessings (If we endure- James 1:12).
- Sermon #1–A Source of Death. (If we fail to Endure- James 1:15)

- Sermon # 2- The Source of Temptations. (God or the Devil? -James 1:13) (1 Corinthians 10:13)
- Sermon #3- The Role of Desire in Our Temptation. (James1: 14)
- Sermon #4 -The Process of Temptation. (James 1:14-15)
- Sermon #5 -What Happens When Desire and Enticement Meet? (James 1:13-14)
- Sermon #6 -When Sin is Conceived It Has to Give Birth. (unless we perform a spiritual abortion James 1:14-15)
- Sermon #7 -What Happens When Sin Grows Up? (James 1:15)

The sermon series above was used on Sunday mornings, and Bible study groups in mid-week to fine tune them. Additional Scriptures such as Romans chapters 6 and 8; and Genesis 4 were used, in an attempt to understand the obstacle that sin has played in buffering church renewal. It took some time before fruit of renewal in this area became visible, eventually behavioral change towards one another became evident, and marriages and relationships were improved. Laziness, selfishness and other character defects were targets of intentional change. Discipleship, while it may not eradicate sin, it allows the believer to become aware, confess and escape its bondage. The awareness of sin and its effects made renewal possible.

As the unleashing of spirituality took place within the congregation, CBF began to contemplate which direction God would move them to next. Knowing that as disciples of Jesus Christ they were called to live a life and pattern of love, not only in the church, but also in the community. Somehow they must engage the community with this new found love. Now that we have discussed the grounds and work for spiritual formation, we will look at how that spiritual formation allowed CBF to incarnate itself in the mission of God.

Chapter Four

Small Church / Missional Church

The Mission of God

In this chapter we will review how the small church engages the mission of God. In order for the small urban church to be truly effective, it must understand, submit and seek out the mission of God through Christ Jesus.

It is in this mission that the church's role in community is fulfilled. Fulfillment does not come from programs or outreach, but rather from joining Christ in mission as the church represents God. We will review how CBF a small urban congregation found its fulfillment not in numbers but in obeying the command of Christ to be sent. We will examine the *missio* Dei in its historical context and its present activity in the 21st century urban church.

In order for us to understand the mission of God, identifying some key words and ideas would be helpful. It is best that we start with the word mission and the term *missio* Dei. After World War I at the Brandenburg Missionary Conference in 1932, Karl Barth articulated missions as an activity of God himself. Using the term *actio* Dei, Barth suggested that the Trinitarian relationship within the Godhead is the source of all mission. The following year (1933) German missiologist Karl Hartenstien expressed similar views. However, rather than using the term *actio* Dei, a term coined by Barth, he employed the term *missio* Dei, the mission of God. This concept of *missio* Dei suggest that from eternity past the triune God has been on a mission. To fulfill that mission, He engages in a series of sending acts. The Father sent the Son into the world at the Incarnation (John 1:14).

The Father guides the Son during the Son's ministry (5:31). The Son sends the church into the world after the resurrection (20:21). The Son sent the Spirit into the world at Pentecost (14:16-17; Acts 2:1-4)."[66]

Since the time of Barth, and the many others that subscribe to this view, the words missions and missional have become part of the Christian language. The concepts are not new in any sense, but the usage, terminology and practices appear to have been revived in the 21st century Church language. There are many books written on the subject such as: *Missional Leader, Missional Church, Missional Renaissance, A Field Guide for the Missional Congregation, Church Next.*" [67] These books go into to detail on the missional responsibilities of the church. The old thought of being missional in foreign countries alone, is discussed and brought to light within the biblical narrative of God's mission. These authors reveal, that God's mission is not only abroad, but also very present and active right here in our local communities. Not only are there numerous books and journals written on the missional subject, but there are also seminaries that have adopted the missional language and mindset.

Here are just a few that have missional foci: First there is Biblical Theological Seminary, whose focus is on following Jesus into the world. Then there is Northern Theological Seminary, whose focus is on forming pastors to lead the church into mission. Nazarene Theological Seminary, is another, having long supported and engaged the idea of the Bible being a missional narrative.

Missional theology is present in our institutions and the church of modernity has adopted missional thought and practice. This missional mind set has open doors for the church to join in the *missio* Dei.

Darrell Guder describes this revival of missional thought and practice as a "reorientation of our theology."[68] Seeing and speaking of God in missional language provide better ways for evangelizing. This happens when the church assist people in seeing that God is present in their situation regardless of their condition. It is then that a view of God, that has not yet been reveal, will shine through. The change of imagination that God is just not in the church house, but also present in communities across the world, gives hope to the downtrodden and those that are forgotten by the larger society. This reorientation provides a fresh theological awakening towards God."[69]

In the missional church, Jesus sends followers into the world where the Father is already at work. The *missio* Dei invites the church to join God in the world. This is a major shift in the way some churches think. Some subscribe to the idea, that the only way to connect to God is in the church building itself, through its communal worship practices. That is not to say that we should neglect communal worship, for (Hebrews 10:25) warns against such. Instead realizing that God is active and present in the community as well. This will allow us to see a much broader reality of God's love for humanity.

The Western view of Christianity in the 21st century is slowly arousing from a slumber of an inward view of God, to an awareness of God's missional plan of redemption. This redemption is seen in an outward manifestation of God's love in community, through the sending agents of Jesus Christ. We do well not to forget, that in the Great Commission, the church is the sent agent. Sent to join God in the world, and not take God into the world. Actually we are sent to demonstrate God's presence and love for all.

Rodman MacIlvaine III writes "The concept of missions is not primarily the activity of the church, but of God. The emphasis is not that Jesus gave the church a mission, rather, the emphasis is that Jesus invited the church into God's preexisting mission."[70]

The British bishop and theologian Lesslie Newbigin's writing on the *missio* Dei, reveals that the life blood of the church is in its being sent. The doctrine of the Bible is God the Father sending the Son, and God the Father and the Son sending the Spirit.

But he does not stop there as Barth did, he expands the view to include yet another movement in Scripture. This movement is of the Father, Son, and Holy Spirit sending the church into the world. By extending the mission of the Father to the church, it allows the church to understand that it is an agent that was sent by a higher authority and not of itself. The mission of God gives direction and instruction on what the church should be doing in the world. Newbigin's view also gives the church identity with God, and purpose for existence."[71]

The *missio* Dei, is a command to join God in mission by continuing Christ's mission in the world, the very mission in which he died for. Now if the Father sends the Son and Spirit, and the Son sends the church, then the church must to submit to the mission of God, and seek out God's activity in communities. The question one might ask is what is a missional church? What does a missional church look like?

MacIlvaine in What Is the Missional Church Movement? writes "A missional church is a unified body of believers, intent on being God's missionary presence to the indigenous community that surrounds them, recognizing that God is already at work. Taking seriously the fact that they have been sent by the risen Christ to be the agents of God's preexisting mission, missional churches embrace a distinctly countercultural mindset."[72]

The missional church expresses the love of God to the world. It identifies God's intent and commitment to the redeeming of humanity. Because God is on mission, and we are made in the image of God, we too are sent on mission also. Churches large and small all share the same redemptive mission. Expressing to the world, love, grace and mercy of the almighty God."[73]

Where Is God

CBF had not yet come to the understanding of what it meant to be a missional church. Some of the leadership team spent nearly four years in missional training at seminary, learning to read the Bible with a missional mindset. They would rely on this training to steer them towards missional thinking, while experiencing scriptures through the triuneness of a missional God. This missional training helped the leadership to understand what missional would mean in the 21st century community. In order to embrace missional theology and practices, it required that CBF recognize their calling as agents of Christ, sent out into the world.

Being sent into the world, the congregation started its missional journey by connecting to the community through prayer walks. On these walks congregants would stop and engage the community in conversations about their relationship with God.

On one such occasion the family was asked how do they see God, and do they think that he is present? Their view of God acknowledged that He does exist, but God's presence was described as distant and detached. They asked such questions as: Why would God allow people to live like this? Why do God allow young kids to get shot? Why would God allow the abuse of babies? Not quite sure where this worldview was coming from, the congregation could only guess that it was the result of economic injustices and hardships. Included in these hardships were joblessness, poor housing, lack of education, and addictions, just to name a few.

Sin played a major role in their worldview even if they did not understand it at this time. Because of sin, there is a need for the risen Savior. Sin is the catalyst for the mission of God.

To try and get a better understanding of church and community, the leadership team then turned towards the congregation. The leadership asked the congregation, how do "they" see God in the community? Surprisingly their answer was not very different at all. They too questioned God's presence and activity in the community. Their conclusions were based on what the congregation perceived as a community lack of spiritual interest. What they saw was senseless violence, and in some instances, a community built on self-destruction and without hope. The leadership team was at a standstill, not knowing which way to go. With a congregation whose mindset was not much different than the people God had sent them after, the question remained, where were they to go from here? Once again CBF returned to prayer, seeking discernment on where and how God wanted them to join in mission.

Since each context is different, God's activity and presence will present itself in very diverse ways. Congregations must therefore continue to ask themselves "What is God up to in their context? Once they determine what God is up to in their communities, they can then seek out what God desires them to do in that context.

The urban response to what God is doing probably will look a little different than the rural response, although God is the Creator of all. Danger exists when churches attempt to join God's mission based on the context of others." [74] This will cause them to have a distorted view of what God may look like. Because God rules all of culture, He reveals Himself differently to each.

The contextualization of the urban African American Church is not a 21st century phenomenon, each culture and denomination has found its place and context in which to view the grace of God and our risen Savior. Richard Allen establish the Bethel Chapel African Methodist Episcopal Church in Philadelphia in 1794. Then there is the Abyssinian Baptist Church of Harlem, steep in tradition of the old negro spirituals, which is, until this day, their context for experiencing God. Then there are the numerous storefront churches, now typical of non-denominational congregations.

All which see God based on their context. In the same way the small church must see God in its context and not the context of the larger congregations."[75]

CBF desired to know, what was God up to in their context? And what did God want them to do? To get this information the leadership team used the tool of prayer walks. On these walks through the community the congregation learned how to see through the spiritual senses.

It was easy to walk and make assumptions based on what they might have seen with their natural senses. But the leadership asked them to walk and pray in the Spirit, and listen for the voice of the Spirit. What was the Spirit saying to them? Were there signs of love, peace, hope, kindness, joy?

The teams involved in the prayer walks would often reassemble at the church and share what the Lord had shown each team or individual. It was a surprising discovery how the teams were able to see God's presence in community, and hear God's speaking to them. God's presence was shown in various ways. The mother speaking of hope, while feeding her infant, praying that God would make a better life for her and her child. Then there was the family that stopped one team, and asked for prayers for the entire family. Many asked the team where the church was and if they could pray for children that were facing the judicial system for criminal charges. Some spoke of the desire to attend church once they got themselves together.

There were definite signs that God was at work in this community. There were also street *philosophers* who readily and willing engage teams in conversations, while affirming their absolute aware-ness of the one and only true God. Even in the midst of indulging in drug activity, they spoke of the need for help from God.

This group was asked if they believed that God existed? And if so, then why engage in drug activity? The response was, "they believed that God wanted them to make it the best way they could." They then stated that "society has left them no other choice and, as long as they are not hurting anyone physically, then God was okay with what they were doing." They were then challenged on what their activity was doing to the community. To the team's amazement they willing engaged in conversation, and did not mind being challenged on what they believed.

McIlvaine writes "when the church is sent by Christ, on one hand they engage a lifestyle of common ground with the world but without moral or spiritual compromise. On the other hand, they are not afraid to challenge assumptions, even the idols within the culture that harm enslave people."[76]

If the church is going to see the activity of God in a given com-munity or cultural context, it cannot be afraid to engage those that are present. This engagement will allow the church to see where God is working, and provide a glimpse into the lives of those being transformed.

Engaging the community on common ground, allowed the church to not only see where God is, but also reassured the church that God has preceded them and is already at work in their context. W. Rodman MacIlvaine conveys this sentiment as well. That God precedes us in mission and the Holy Spirit is already at work convicting unbelievers of their need for salvation. Our role in joining God in mission does not required that we attempt to do any "soul saving," but rather allow God to do what only He can do. We needed only to be instruments in God's missional plan."[77]

To the small church, the idea of a preceding, strong and present God, is very liberating, and encouraging. This is especially true, when there is a lack of numbers and resources. The church should understand that redemption is God's work, and all that is needed, is to come along side of this active work in the lives of unbelievers and those who have gone astray.

Embracing the fact, that God precedes the church and is present and active in community will give the church courage to face the daily task of coping with the drug abuse in urban areas. A walk down inner-city streets will reveal the story of a society that is filled with hopelessness, hunger, poverty, and excessive violence. These communities reveal babies that are born to crack addicted mothers.

Families that are attempting to come to grips with drug related murders of one or more siblings. These and many other abuses present a dismal picture to the church. And if the church does not embrace the preceding presence of God in their communities, fear can immobilize them from joining God in mission.

To know that God is already in the city and waiting for the church, gives congregations the strength and courage to confront the ills of society."[78] The urban church can rest in the power of a strong and preceding God, with confidence in God's ability to transform communities. The size of the small church is not a factor in the mission of God, after all, it is God's strength and power, that delivers and set free.

It is God who ordained the mission, it is God who precedes the church in mission, and it is God who will do the supernatural work in the hearts of humanity. To know that God goes before us and is waiting on the church to join Him, should ultimately strengthen our resolve to carry out the great commission found in (Matthew 28) regardless of a churches size or resources.

When the small church embraces the missional call, as God's mission, and rest in God's preceding presence, they can be effective in communities where Christ has sent them. Jim Kitchens writes "The church is not the goal of God's mission, but its instrument; that is the church is the means, not the end of God's purposes." [79] Kitchens gives great insight to the church, providing an opportunity to abandon the old adage of "If you build it, they will come." It is with this mentality that western culture continues to build bigger and larger congregations hoping that people will come and fill its auditoriums.

Instead a sensitivity to being sent is needed, so that the pursuit will change, as the church runs to meet God in the fields of urban harvest. This change in thinking will liberate the small church to see itself as Gods see it. The missional church measures their effectiveness, not by counting the number of people attending weekly service, but by assessing how effectively they serve in the missional activity of God."[80]

This is one of the reason why small churches, urban and rural can be effective in their context. Small churches can gain strength from the *missio* Dei as they embrace their calling to be sent onto the mission field, joining the activity of God. This knowledge of *missio* Dei can change the view of worship and put to rest, the counting of sheep that many pastors and church leaders often succumb to.

A better understanding of the mission of God can change the way communal worship is celebrated. Missional Christians view corporate worship as a time to celebrate God's eternal mission in the world. This communal worship is also a time to strengthen their role in God's mission, so that they can continue to live effectively for Christ. The corporate worship service is intentional as they purpose to connect with each other, while ministering to the corporate body, as they are equipped – not entertained."[81]

Christ's sending the church into the world was one thing, but connecting to the larger community is another. Before CBF could join God in mission, they need to first understand this new community they have been sent to.

An Invitation from God

The leadership turned to a congregational study of Scot McKnight's *The Jesus Creed*."[82] This book was chosen because the central theme of loving God and neighbor is missional in nature.

Pastor Mike had the privilege to take a class with the author Scot McKnight and learned how useful the teaching would be for his context. After reading the Jesus Creed, the leadership team agreed that the book would be helpful in gaining insights on how to join God missionally by engaging the community as neighbors.

This study was pivotal in understanding how to engage God's people, particularly those that were on the fringes of society. McKnight challenges how the church views those that are outcast. Did the congregation see them as community? Were they outcasts or neighbors?

The Jesus Creed discusses in detail the history of the Jewish tradition as it relates to the Shema and the Torah. The Shema is an affirmation of Judaism and a declaration of faith in one God, that is found within the Torah. This affirmation if it were summed up could read: Love God by Living the Torah. This can be seen in (Deuteronomy 6:4-5) where the Lord God is one, and must be love with heart, soul and strength. Then Jesus comes along and adds to the Shema/Torah from (Leviticus 19:18) to "Love your neighbor as yourself." [83]

This represented a major problem for some of the Jewish people. Not only must they love God with heart, soul and strength, and love their neighbor as themselves, but this meant loving people with different cultural practices, people who ate non-kosher foods, and had a lifestyle that may have been different than theirs. They also must love God by following Jesus.

This creed has now become a stumbling block of offense to some Jews. This amendment to the Torah, introduced by Jesus, is filled with missional character. The 21st century church must love God in the same way, while loving neighbors as they love themselves and be willing to follow God into urban and rural communities across the globe. The truth of this is, following Jesus will lead pastors to large church ministries and many more pastors to small congregational service.

McKnight writes "A scribe asks Jesus about the essence of spiritual formation, and Jesus gives him and old answer with a revolutionary twist: Love God and love others, and love God by following me. The scribe realizes that he will need to re-center everything."[84] This is the same conclusion that the church of modernity must arrived at. We must re-center our lives within the *missio* Dei. Truly Christ was sending CBF to love and follow God into community, to share God's great love, with those who were neighbors, and not just potential church members.

At the time of Jesus, table customs could be used to measure one's commitment to the Torah. People were often reprimanded and might even be treated as outcast, if they ate with those who were not Jewish, or food that was not kosher. But for Jesus the table was a place of inclusion and not exclusion. The table was a place of fellowship and acceptance. This can be seen in (Mark 2:14-17) where

Jesus table customs are called into question by some of the Jewish leaders. Jesus's inclusion to the table, of tax collectors and sinners did not follow the Jewish way of Torah behavior. Loving God was not a major stumbling block for the Jews, when done the way that they were accustomed to. But Jesus challenged them to a new kind of love, one that included their neighbors. Another twist in this is that they must love neighbors as they love themselves. This meant that to love God, is to love others in a way, that they too can be accepted at the table."[85]

This hit CBF really hard, because they realized that there were some neighbors who felt they had no place or right at the table of God, because of their sins.

There were also some neighbors that the congregation did not really love as they loved themselves. McKnight writes "Jesus invites to the table those who are spiritually and socially sick, because Jesus can heal." [86]

This study helped to revolutionized the leadership and congregational thinking, as the realization set in, that God was at work in this small church preparing a table for their neighbors. Christ had literally sent CBF into the community to extend invitations to the table, to enjoy a free banquet of love, forgiveness, mercy and healing. CBF had to see the community as its neighbors and love them as they love themselves. That means inviting and accepting them to the table as they were.

CBF envisioned what dining with Christ at the table could do in the lives of their neighbors. This acceptance to the table eliminated boundaries and feelings of alienation while opening the door to fellowship. Just as the table created a new society in the time of Jesus, it also creates a new society in the 21st century."[87]

As part of continual spiritual formation, the leadership felt a need to not only glean from books by various authors, but to spend time gleaning from the word of God. In missional training they had learned the spiritual discipline of listening to God through the written word. This was done through a practice learned at Biblical Theological Seminary (Missional Theology Class) called "Indwelling in The Word."

In this process one person read the Scriptures, then each individual would read it on his or her own silently. After that, a discussion of what Spirit has said to each person would ensue. It was amazing to hear what the Spirit was saying through the corporate body as they engaged the written word. The congregation was actually reading Scripture and expecting to hear from God.

They learned that God does speak to them too, and not just the pastor! CBF practiced indwelling in the word on such passages (Luke 11:1-4). Here the disciples of Jesus asked Him to "teach them to pray as John also taught his disciples." They examined in detail the Master's response.

One of the things that the Spirit revealed corporately was the wording "Thy Kingdom Come." Questions began to surface, as to exactly what the Kingdom of God look like in the community? Missional thought had begun to form the way CBF interpret Scripture. The kingdom of God, is the society in which the will of God is established to transform all of life. It is more than what is happening in their personal lives, but rather what God is doing in all of creation to accomplish the redemptive plan. The kingdom of God transforms relationships between God, self and others."[88]

Missional leaders must keep focused toward a kingdom agenda that includes the church but extends to the world. The focus of church leadership and congregations must be on how to engaged those outside the church with the kingdom agenda. That agenda is displayed in acts of mercy, kindness, love and justice. The kingdom transforms, heals and suffers long."[89]

The kingdom or reign of God can be seen in the way the church serves. When the church serves in love and obedience to the will of God, then that service is a sign of God's reign.

The church then embodies the kingdom agenda, and the kingdom that has come, is now being accessed. The Kingdom of God is something to be lived out in a continuous fashion, as we look more and more like Christ."[90]

Alan J. Roxburgh writes in *Missional: Joining God in The Neighborhood*, "The Spirit is out there ahead of us, inviting us to listen as creation groans in our neighborhoods. Only in the willingness to risk entering, dwelling, eating, and listening, will we stand a chance as the church to bring the embodied Jesus to the world." [91]

Roxburgh views the Spirit as a missional agent sent by God ahead of the church, preparing hearts and minds to receive the embodied love of Christ. When the church yields to the Spirit, the Kingdom reign can become visible and realized in the hearts of humanity.

Thy kingdom come, can be viewed as a continuous reign of the missional God. Jesus reveals this Kingdom reign in the inauguration speech found in (Luke 4:18-19). Here we can see that Jesus embodies the kingdom and is present to transform the lives of the poor, brokenhearted, captives, blind and oppressed. One can suggests that the living out of God's redemptive plan, can constitute God's Kingdom coming on earth as it is in heaven. The more the church is transformed, the more the kingdom will be visible, in essence it will continue coming until it is revealed in totality in Christ's return to earth."[92]

Joel Hunt sees the coming of God's Kingdom as *God's Rule*. "Thy Kingdom come refer to the coming of God's Kingdom and mean that God is to rule.

It means that God is to rule not at some future time or in some far-away place, but now, in this day, and over the people of our times." [93]

God's Kingdom rule is a continuous rule over a present people, which allows us to view the kingdom, as a constant present and ever revealing, until at last it presents itself in the conclusion of the redemptive plan.

Gordon Lund writes in *Thy Kingdom Come* "Christ is the Kingdom as well as the king. People are in Him or they are not in the kingdom."[94] Lund suggests that people cannot build the kingdom for God because he is the Kingdom, and when we understand this then we can act as agents for the kingdom, bringing the lost into the kingdom. Not in an eschatological sense, but in a present sense, leading to the eschatological reign of Christ.

The question now faced by the small church is: is the small church willing to invite the disenfranchised, into the ruling reign of God's Kingdom, through Jesus Christ?

To be an effective small church ministry, they must ask themselves this question. This means that the invitation must be delivered bodily, through intentional acts of love and kindness. The small church must be willing to act experimentally and with flexibility, in its worship practices, and community involvement. The church must engage a community with certain vulnerability, and a heart to love the sinner, while denouncing the sin."[95] When the church acts in this fashion we are representatives of the kingdom, regardless of congregational size, resources or location.

As redeemed representatives, we are called to serve as 'Eikons.' that is, humans representing the image of God.

McKnight describes an Eikon as "God-oriented, self-oriented, other-oriented. To be an Eikon is to be a missional being- one designed to love God, self and others and to represent God by participating in Gods rule in this world." [96]

The church is charged with the task of revealing the imago Dei, in the flesh to the world (the same way Christ brought God's redemptive plan to the world in the flesh).

When Eikons participate in the *missio* Dei, it signifies a willingness to engage in relationship with the larger community. CBF knew that they were representatives of God's Kingdom, and that they need a way to connect to the community to extend invitation into the rule, love, mercy, and grace of God.

We will discuss in our next chapter how the church can connect to the community and submerge itself in God's missional plan for the community.

Chapter Five

Connecting to Community

Finding God in Community

N ow that we have discovered that God is on mission and calls us to join Him, we will map out ways to connect to communities where the Spirit of God is active. If the church is going to join God in mission, they must learn how to connect with the community in which God is sending them. In this chapter we will explore ways the CBF congregation connected to the neighborhood in which they existed. In connecting to the community, the church can then find out where God is active and working in the lives of people. It is our hope that this chapter will guide small urban churches through the successes and pit falls of connecting to community.

Finding God in community would not be done through church services or behind church walls. It would include all of the spiritual disciplines that CBF had learned over the past six years. As they studied the sounds and language that has been frequently used in the community. When someone would speak of the Kensington community, it was never in endearing terms. Very seldom was the word community used among its residents.

Sometimes, the word neighborhood would be used, mostly in community activist circles, but not with the residents of Kensington. The leadership began to question if this was a community, neighborhood or just a group of people in a geographical location living independently of each other. This lack of community could exist for many reasons. Some might say that as African Americans began to progress and attain better employment, they departed from the urban communities they once called home.

This resulted in an instability in the neighborhoods. It also broke the bonds with lifelong friends and families. This ultimately resulted in others moving into the community with no ties or familial history, creating a communication gap, as people interacted less and less.

Diana Bass in *Grounded: Finding God in The World A Spiritual Revolution suggests*: People create neighborhoods when they gather together beyond family ties, live close to others, and choose to share certain resources (schools, stores, electricity, roads). Neighborhoods are born when people settle in a certain geographical space and turn it, in common effort with others, into a habitual place." [97] Although Bass's definition of neighborhood resembled the Kensington community in theory, however, "Kenso's" as they are commonly called, did not speak of it that way, nor behave in like manner. Instead the only resources shared, were the public school system, and stores and roads. Even in a celebratory spirit such as the community block parties, sharing was at a minimum, and it was a gathering of a group of individual celebrations, and not the communal celebration that it should be.

Walter Kloetzli and Arthur Hillman in *Urban Church Planning* writes "In spite of the large numbers of persons about him the urban citizen may have even fewer intimate relationships with other persons than do members of the smaller rural societies. His travel, his shopping, his amusements, and even his work are often carried on in the midst of total strangers." [98]

Because of these independent lifestyles, urban neighborhoods are at a disadvantage. This can cause communities like Kensington, to be blinded to the presence of God's love within a neighborhood.

As the CBF congregation continued to listen to the sounds in the community, the word they heard daily from residents was "hood." This word reflects the feelings and emotions of how they felt about their community. It is often used in African American communities, and in urban environments globally. The American Heritage College Dictionary defines hood as "Slang, A neighborhood, usually in the inner city, African American Vernacular for neighborhood." It has the connotation of the Ghetto, an impoverished neglected or otherwise disadvantaged residential area of a city. Usually refer to urban or inner city life. This debased view of community will eventually descend into hopelessness, and an urgency to move into a community with views of being neighborly, complete with neighborhood associations will soon drive them to abandon the inner city communities.

After much discussion CBF, knew that if they were going to find God in their neighborhood, they would have to view the residents not as individuals, but rather as a connected group of people that God was transforming into community. CBF somehow would have to put the "neighbor" back into the word "hood." To do this, would recreate the word neighborhood, and help them to see, that God was present and active in the neighborhood.

Throughout the biblical narrative God often worked in and through communities of people. Bass writes "If God dwells within our individual households, then certainly God dwells next door as well. God abides with us as a gathered community of neighbors. When we live near others, even with only the thinnest of personal connections, we will still belong through the environment we share." [99]

In Matthew 22:37-40 Jesus commands that we love God, and our neighbor as ourselves. If Jesus commands us to love our neighbors as ourselves, then surely where there is love, there is Jesus Himself. So if God was going to be found in community, it would be where there is loving and caring for one another. In essence God can be found in the missional activity of divine love in community.

Bass echoes this sentiment that neighborly relationships are in the nucleus of divine love, and help us to understand the existence of God. It is in this existence that we can rest assured, wherever God exists, the Holy Spirit's activity in the lives of humanity is present." [100] The bottom line is the activity of God, is the activity of love that flows through us and outward to mankind. The activity of God is so powerful and gracious that it transcends race, gender, social and economic status, and even global locations. This can be seen in the many disasters of the 21st century. Such disasters include the attack on the World Trade Center, the tsunami in Indonesia, the earthquake in Haiti and the Syrian refugees attack, just to name a few. The global community joined in the activity of God's love as one, comforting, praying, crying, caring, rescuing, and sharing in the lives of those affected.

In order to find God in community, CBF would have to take responsibility for the community, by seeing them and treating them as neighbors. Not only must they see the community as neighbors but also love them as those within the congregation. No longer could the congregation sit back and wait for the them to find Jesus, but with vigor and determination CBF, must demonstrate the love of God on common ground. In (John 1:14) John declares that "The Word became flesh and dwelt among us."

In the same way the congregation must connect to the community, by having its presence in the neighborhood (not just the church service or building). This connection must have a foundation of compassion for a neighborhood that is in desperate search and need of the love of Christ. McKnight suggests, that engaging the community in empathy as it experiences trials, joys, and sadness, will enable the church to act compassionately. Compassion is a life style and not an independent event." [101] Through this type of engagement, the church connects with the community in a way that they become part of it. Without this empathy and compassion, they will never be invited to enter into the grief and death of the community's sons and daughters, to bring kingdom healing.

The small church needs to understand that despite its size, it has been given the ministry of reconciliation. God has called the church to represent Him in the world, continuing the restoring work of Jesus Christ. God brings healing through this reconciling effort of the church and the world. The African American tradition has a long history of dealing with community pain and sorrow with the church being at the center of their anguish and joy. This history of pain is ongoing as families deal with the senseless killing of African American sons.

Today the Black urban church is where symposiums are held in hopes to extinguish the fire and anger that burns within urban communities across the globe. When the church connects to the community it provides a spiritual power that can allow healing to take place.

Stephen Rasor and Christine Chapman in *Black Power From The Pew* suggest: The African Americans function in such a way in community, that through spirituality they can experience liberation in the face of severe suffering and pain.

The view that God is in the midst of their traumatic experiences has enabled the African American community to triumph in dignity and liberation in unbelievable circumstances. Through this God centered and God present spirituality they are able to claim sorrow and express their joy." [102]

It is with this spirituality that the urban church finds it connectedness in our neighborhood and communities. Form the slums of New York to the projects of Philadelphia, in the barrios of east LA, and the ghettos of West Africa. The voice of God calls the church out of the pew in into these communities. The Spirit directs engagement through indigenousness churches, that embody Christ in their thinking, actions and love.

The Small Indigenous Church

CBF understood that in order to join God in mission, its indigenous nature must be more than its physical location in the community. To be truly indigenous, the congregation must immerse itself within the community, and take on its shape character and form. This must be done without compromising biblical ethos. Indigenous churches for the most part, are churches suited to local culture and led by local Christians. How to become indigenous would be a trial and error especially in an unpredictable community as Kensington, a community where the turnover rate in residency is usually one to three years. Through much prayer and fasting the congregation sought God, in how they could engage the community without compromising the gospel. Before this could become a congregational effort, a pastoral and leadership view must first take shape and form.

Edward Wimberley in African American Pastoral Care uses the word village to refer to community. He writes "The village is that small communal network of persons linked together by a common biological, family, cultural heritage living in a particular geographical location where frequent interaction is a reality." [103]

The leadership team struggled with how to engage this village of family and neighbors. It was decided that the only way to engage the village as Wimberley calls it, was to immerse themselves in it. The following case studies will reveal a firsthand account and context of the Kensington community. They will further serve as pastoral missional reflections and a source of hope for small urban churches in communities experiencing similar circumstances. The case studies will reflect an action model as they reveal the spiritual transformations experienced by CBF in their calling to be sent. While there are many case studies that can be added to this project, the studies mentioned were chosen because of the author's direct involvement, and how it has affected his life. This will bring us to our first case study on being an indigenous small church community.

Case Study 1- Pastoral and Congregational Care

Pastor Mike met Gloria (not her real name) as she left her porch and walked over to where he was playing football and introduced herself. She expressed to him that she had never seen a church play football during Sunday service hours. She stated that most churches just go inside and never become involved in the community. Through conversation Pastor Mike learned about her family and that she was a single mother and grandmother with a troubled son. Her daughter had recently lost her child's father due to gun violence.

She became more and more comfortable as the Pastor allowed her to tell and retell her story as many times as she liked and as many ways as she liked. He also shared some of his stories with her, and some of the similarities gave them commonality. This allowed for a friendship, and soon a neighborly relationship. After the initial meeting Pastor Mike saw that she was reluctant to come into the church, but was often willing and ready to engage him in conversation whenever the two would encounter one another in the community. Gloria often filled Pastor Mike in on the events of the community, such as crime, deaths and neighborhood parties. She also filled him in on her life's events as well.

It was a warm summer's day, as he sat on the church steps to take in the sights, sounds and smells of the community as was his custom, when Gloria called out to him in anger and tears. As he approached her, he asked her what was the issue, she explained to him, that her son had become violent and ask if he would talk with him before she called the police. Knowing that this situation could very easily get out of hand as he was hostile, Pastor Mike prayed and asked God for guidance and entered the house, and allowed the young man to have an avenue to tell his story.

Attending to his story (by acknowledging his pain and anger as he shared), gave him an audience that he so desperately needed. Pastor Mike also shared some similarities from his life as a youth growing up in urban Philadelphia, as a way to connect with him. The young man's anger subsided and he was given assurance that God loved him, and that there was a better way to handle what he was dealing with. He decided to get dressed and leave the house and stay with a friend for a while. Satisfied at the temporary outcome, even though some behavioral, and psychological counseling to come along side of it will be necessary.

Shortly after his departure Gloria began to express that she was surprised that he would talk to Pastor Mike because he was very bitter against the church. Eventually Pastor Mike counseled with Gloria's son again, but he soon left the community and move down south with family members. When asked why he was bitter with the church, she explained that prior to CBF's arrival to that church building, her nephew, her son's cousin raped a little girl inside of the church and the leadership of the church testified against him in court.

The offender is currently serving time in prison, and it is this reason that the community's heart was hardened against the church. Pastor Mike explained to her that what her nephew did was wrong, and that the church had to obey God's law as well as the law of the land. She also agreed that it was a criminal act. Pastor Mike made a point to run into her as much as possible, to keep open the lines of communication and provide pastoral care.

A revelation had taken place in Pastor Mike, the church would become indigenous through pastoral and congregational care. Indigenous care, happens in and outside of the church building. Care for the community could take place outside the church setting, and had nothing to do with membership or who came inside the church.

God was calling the small congregation to provide care for the community and invite them into kingdom love.

The small church is not small after all. But like a good shepherd the church must seek out the lost, and mend their wounds leading them back to the fold. The small church is sent by Jesus, into the world, just like the larger churches are. And their numerical size or resources are not a factor in submitting to the mission of Christ.

Pastor Mike explained to Gloria, that although her nephew was in jail, God can and will forgive him for his sins. They continued their conversations as Pastor Mike reassured her that God has a purpose for this community and her life. Over a year's time, he asked Gloria to become the block captain, with the support of the church, and she agreed. This provided several opportunities for the church to become neighbors, and not just a people who showed up on Sunday morning for service.

Connecting to the community also provided an environment for caring and sharing in community. Slowly, CBF began to understand that their small church congregation was larger than those that came to worship on Sunday. The small Kensington congregation was a village congregation, and they had the privilege to care for the entire community. The care extended to those that did not come to communal worship and those that did. God's missional activity was within the congregation, and seen in its transformations. God's love was also in community, using the church as a vessel to demonstrate agape love for the Kensington community.

The congregation took personal responsibility for being sent by Christ, in community and became intentional in connecting and living indigenously. This was seen as they engaged the community by spending time on different stoops talking with those that did and did not attend the church. The focus was not in inviting people to a church service, but rather a concern and care about the things that were happening in the community and in their lives. The more the congregation engaged the community, they began to identify with the Pastor and the congregation as their spiritual care givers, even though they still had not yet come to faith.

On one prayer walk, the congregation was completely amazed at how many residents in the community acknowledge the church, as belonging to the neighborhood, and assured them that they would be attending soon. It was then that CBF realized, that the small church has really grown outside of the few that attended Sunday morning worship. In (John 10:16 NKJV) Jesus states "And other sheep I have which are not of this fold; them also I must bring, and they will hear My voice; and there will be one flock and one shepherd." This resonated within the hearts of the congregation as they pondered this as the reason for being sent by Jesus into the community. Romans 10:14 outlines just how this is to take place. Here Paul writes "How then shall they call on Him in whom they have not believed? And how shall they believe in Him of whom they have not heard? And how shall they hear without a preacher? And how shall they preach unless they are sent?

The small church is one of the agents that God has sent, and must realize that they are on mission to bring God's voice, to the lost sheep. Joining God in mission means that the small church must see themselves not as a small, insignificant, under resourced, a minimal body of believers, but rather and important part of God's great missional plan. Reaching sheep that only they can reach. CBF outreach programs must be free and clear of any intentions, for membership recruiting. Its focus would be on brining the voice and love of God, to the community, without any expectations. This has greatly reduced the stress of counting numbers and using attendance as a plumb line for God's activity in the community. Providing this care would take on such forms as providing funerals for free, to those in the community, in need of spiritual care in times of death.

Case Study 2- Soul Care

Mrs. Sanchez approached the congregation one day and shared about her 29-year-old son who was in a coma and they were going to remove him from life support. He was in prison for the last 10 years and had a seizure resulting in a coma.

She asked if the church could visit him at the hospital and pray for him, as she did not have a pastor. Never having met Mrs. Sanchez before the day she approached him, Pastor Mike asked how did she find out about the church? She then stated that her grandson attended the youth group at the church, and that she did not know where else to turn since she did not have a church home. Mrs. Sanchez stated that she used to belong to a Pentecostal church a long time ago but had fallen off and quit attending church all together. She further stated that she attended a church service at CBF before and liked the welcomed experience she received. So Pastor Mike went to see her son and provided pastoral care for him and the entire family.

Mrs. Sanchez and family had to make a hard decision to take him off of life support and asked if Pastor Mike would be present. While administering care throughout the process, Pastor Mike began to share the love of Jesus for hat family even in a time of sorrow. CBF also demonstrated this love by performing the funeral free of charge. Because he was so young the church was at standing room only capacity during the funeral and as a result of the church's care for the family, a long lasting relationship was formed with the entire family. This relationship allowed the church to enter into the lives of this family as they endured, hardships, joys, divorce, and teen troubles.

Truly God's loving kingdom is present, through this small church that is willing to yield, to being sent by Christ.

Being sent by Christ does not mean that we will always be sent into environments that are pleasant. The small church must not be afraid engage situations that may not be pleasant to the five senses. We must look beyond the exterior and join God in the stench of human life that is produced by sin. Many urban residents that live on the fringes of society are often shunned, even by well-meaning Christians, when they are faced with the physical engagement of lost sheep. This brings us to our next case study of loving beyond the five senses.

Case Study 3-Care Beyond the Five Senses

Carol (not her real name) walked into the sanctuary and asked if there were any clothes that she could have. It was evident that she was very intoxicated and urinated on herself. Her clothes were soiled and she still carried the bottle of alcohol in her hand. From her appearance one could see that drugs and alcohol had taken its toll on her life. Some of the congregation immediately took offense to the presence of alcohol in the sanctuary and that Carol, unknown to the congregation would come in on Sunday morning in such a fashion. Redirecting her to another part of the church, she was given some clothing and escorted out the side door. Before she departed Carol asked for prayer, barely able to stand due to intoxication, and then left with her bottle of beer.

Carol came back two weeks later right before the start of the church service. She introduced herself to the Pastor and then asked him for a hug. Soiled with urine, and intoxicated, she stood there for what seem like an eternity as everyone fell silent to see what the Pastor Mike would do. Pastor Mike pondered in his mind, should he hug her? Did he really want to get the smell of urine all over his nice suit? Time seemed suspended as the thoughts raced through his mind. Finally, Pastor Mike hugged her and was given the warmest hug he ever received.

Pastor Mike was very uncomfortable as the congregation watched and escorted her out the building. Throughout the sermon and the coming days Pastor Mike could not get that hug and kiss out of his mind. Carol began to come by every Sunday either before or after service and now she always asked Pastor Mike for a hug. Her appearance and condition had not changed, the smell of alcohol continued to surround her, and clothes were still tattered, but it was something special about those hugs.

The public hugs got more spiritually binding. Pastor Mike was no longer afraid to hug her, but embraced the contact as if he was hugging God. Something was taking place on the soul level that could not be explained.

One night near the end of Bible study Carol came by as they gathered in a circle to close in prayer. After prayer the Bible study was over, and Pastor Mike asked Carol how could he help her. To his surprised she said "I just came by for a hug." She then hugged him and told him that she loved him and left without asking for anything more than a hug. She would see Pastor Mike in the community, and tell everyone that he was her pastor, and then ask for a hug.

Pastor Mike began to inquire in the community about Carol and her story. Information was given that all three of her children had died in a fire and that she began drinking and never was the same again.

There were occasions when she would come to church well groomed, clean clothes, sober and in her right mind and all she wanted was a hug. By this time the relationship had transcended beyond the five senses to a point that whenever Pastor Mike saw her sober or intoxicated, he enjoyed demonstrating and receiving the love of Christ in a simple hug.

When the church regardless of its size, lives in community beyond what they see, hear, feel, taste and smell, the Kingdom of God is present. It is then the community can experience Christ's love and healing that will comfort those who have suffered tragedies beyond what we could imagine. Pastor Mike still has lingering questions. Had Christ sent her to engage the church to help them live beyond the five senses? Was it CBF that needed to experience the kingdom presence?

Edward Wimberley in *African American Pastoral Care* writes "Increased involvement in God's story leads to an increased ability to be concerned about the things that God is concerned about within the church and the world." [104] As the church continues to increase its involvement in the missional story of God, we will gain the ability to care about those that God cares about. Community care also involves strengthening and uniting families. Forging bonds and values that help families remain together as the Spirit work in the lives of people. Joan and Steve are a couple, who have experience care that transcends race into authentic family.

Case Study 4- Caring That Transcends into Authentic Family

Joan (not her real name) lived across the street from the church and would often come to service with her 3 children. When asked her about her husband she said that he did not believe in church. The more she came to church, the CBF congregation got to know her better, while her children became involved in the ministry activities. Mike Jr. who is a police officer, spent time in the after school program helping Joan's 15-year-old daughter with a project for school, he felt that it was something deeper going on with her, and asked Pastor Mike to inquire.

After talking with Joan she revealed that her daughter had been raped by her uncle, and that he was in jail awaiting trial for the crime. This rape had affected the entire family and the grandmother felt that she was at fault because she was at home when the assault happened. The leadership team began to minister to the family by addressing the immediate needs of food and clothing.

This news came during the Christmas holiday season. The church came together and provided toys and food as well as clothing for the family, because of their low income status. Joan and the children continued to attend service and church functions as the congregation provided care. One Sunday she attended church with her live in boyfriend Steve (not his real name).

Pastor Mike engaged him in conversation when the service was over, and could tell that he was hurting inside. Steve came back the next Sunday and said he really enjoyed the service. Pastor Mike had many conversations over the next several months and allowed him an opportunity to share the story of his life and the story of his family's rape incident. Giving him the attention and a chance to be heard is what Steve needed at that time.

Wimberley in *African American Pastoral Care* writes "An indigenous storytelling approach to pastoral care is learned by participating and living in an oral community." [105] When we live in community and connect through oral traditions of attentive speaking and listening, those that have long been without a voice can now be heard. Engaging Steve through attentive listening, and allowing him to speak his own narrative, invited Pastor Mike into his life, community, and world.

Steve was the type of man who loved to fix things, so the church began to work with him as he did odd jobs around the church. Wimberley suggest that true community care enables people to participate meaningfully in life.

Steve was without work and had lost his zest for life. Helping him to find meaning was part of the congregational care plan. CBF allowed Steve to participate in whatever way he was capable around the church, empowering him to take on the role of father, husband and provider. Steve finally yielded to the Holy Spirit and received the gift of salvation. He became a part of the CBF community.

One Sunday Pastor Mike preached a sermon on marriage, and how it was God's plan for the family. After the service Joan and Steve approached Pastor Mike and said that since they had given their lives to Christ they wanted to stop living together and get married. They asked to get married in Pastor Mike's office since they did not have any money for a wedding.

Pastor Mike approached the leadership team and expressed how important it is that CBF become their family and provide a wedding to unite and build the foundation of this family that was already struggling after the rape.

Everyone agreed to the wedding and reception free of charge. When Joan and Steve received the news, they cried and could not believe that an African American church would care about them in such a way (Steve and Joan were Caucasian). The entire congregation served as the wedding party and celebrated the work of the Lord in their lives. Truly God was present in the community, and working through this small church to embody the love of Jesus.

The family immersed themselves into the ministry and the congregation provided care on many different levels. Joan and Steve's daughter had to go to court and face her uncle who had raped her and the family asked Pastor Mike to accompany them because she would not testify if he was not present. Pastor Mike accompanied the family and provided pastoral care just by being present and assuring her that God was with her, and to look directly at Pastor Mike while she was on the witness stand. Spiritual care happens when leaders step into the lives of those in whom they were sent to, affect healing and relief, while empowering, and maturing the individual or families. When the small church realizes this, its effectiveness in the community can reach far beyond a Sunday morning message. Joan and Steve continued to grow and mature in Christ, as Steve began to search for his biological father on the Internet. Steve found him living in Florida, so he and the family moved there and are doing quite well. They found a church home there and are active in the ministry.

The congregation still provides care, that transcends race, gender, and distance. CBF would like to think, the experience they had with the small urban church will go with them throughout all of life.

Through our case studies we have seen ways to connect to the community. Connecting to the community is not always under pleasant circumstances but can be accomplished when we love beyond our five senses. The church must love in a manner that transcends what they feel, see, touch, taste and smell. Not every story will be a success story and there will be people in the missional journey who are hostile to the gospel, and reject offers of help from God's people. Being missional means that the church must be resilient, rather than discouraged in times when their efforts are rebuffed. Through God's grace there are members who are armed police officers, that have helped to secure the safety of the CBF congregation, and the community thus far.

Although limited in resources CBF, perceived through its involvement in the community and the spacious building provided by God, that education would be the arena where God would call them into purposeful mission. This vision to educate the urban youth was not something new to CBF, as it was a vision long before the prospect of owning such a facility came to fruition.

In our next chapter we will explore how a small church with limited resources can join God in mission through praxis of education.

Chapter Six

Rebuilding Community Through Education

The Role of Religious Education

In this chapter we will explore the role of religious education in the urban African American community. Religious education is important to this study because it is the jurisdiction where CBF heard and responded, to the calling of God to act as God's representatives. This chapter will reveal the role of the small church in educating the community in which it is called to serve. In this chapter we will understand the tension of a small church as it seeks to join God in mission, as it experiences the transformation of congregational faith and the unforeseen provisions of God. In this chapter we will experience the struggles and uncertainty of a small church as they learn to trust in the presence and power of God as they live out the kingdom agenda for a community. We will explore how God refocuses a small church that began to operate outside of its abilities.

There is an old African Proverb that says, "It takes a village to raise a child." However, the urban village has become fragmented. This fragmentation is a result of failed government policies and disinvestment in urban communities throughout the world. It is a representation of a society where the disenfranchised has lost hope and prompts many to feel disconnected from the Savior of the world. The urban community in major cities struggles to raise their children in a wholesome environment. This leads to a lack of preparation and skill to navigate a globally diverse world.

Urban families are forced to place their dreams and hopes in a sports contract, or a record deal to make it out of poverty. Unfortunately, getting an NBA or NFL contract only happens for a very small percentage.

The NCCA reports "Many boys and girls grow up dreaming of playing sports in college and the pro ranks. But of the nearly eight million students currently participating in high school athletics in the United States, only 460,000 of them will compete at NCAA schools. And of that group, only a fraction will realize their goal of becoming a professional athlete" [106] The percentage of high school players that actually make it to college and then on to professional sports teams are minuscule. Therefore, educating all youth, especially the urban youth must be a priority for the church community as well as the nation. The chart below gives us some idea of how that breaks down exists in different sport categories. See chart below:

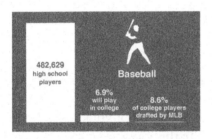

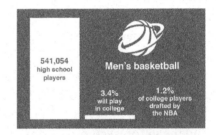

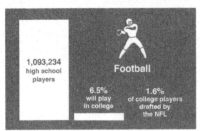

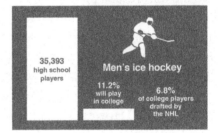

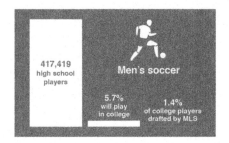
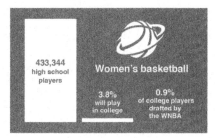

[107] In the mid to late 1960's whatever went on in the African American community, usually happened around or within its religious institutions, whether it was the Black church, Islamic mosques or other spiritual institutions. The Blue Laws were enforced. These laws were designed to restrict or ban some or all Sunday activities for religious reasons. The nation as a whole possessed a certain reverence and respect for the Sabbath day (Sunday). All shopping and business transactions had to be carried out on Saturday because Sunday was a day of worship and family gatherings. Merchants and shopkeepers closed their doors and the taverns ceased to sell alcohol on Sundays, and the focus was on God.

Not everyone attended religious or spiritual institutions, and the Blue Laws created limited and minimal activities in the community when compared to today's opportunities. The Blue Laws had an adverse effect on merchants whose spirituality and religious practices were different than those of the traditional American churches."[108]

The adults that did not attend worship services made sure that their children went to Sunday school to be educated in the biblical narrative. It was the institution of the African American church where formal education began.

The formal education process began long before the African American child entered into pre- school or elementary education. Sunday school, as it was called in the African American tradition and many others, was a vital part of religious education that took place early Sunday mornings. Sunday school ushered in the communal worship day. This religious format of education is still present and effective in urban and mainline churches today.

Children were often questioned by parents at the family dinner table, about the things taught and learned during the Sunday school hour. This gathering of students took place in the sanctuary and throughout the church building. The congregation would be sectioned off by invisible walls, in different areas of the church. This division of the congregation enabled participation in Christian education for the entire family. This included; senior adults, adults, young adults, youth, juniors and children.

Each group was taught by a lay leader within the congregation. The universal curriculum was used by churches across denominational lines, but rarely if ever did this material reflect in its pictures and articles people of African American heritage. The education material instructed in the biblical narrative. The lessons were from Bible stories such as Daniel in the Lion's Den, the story of Jesus Birth, Burial and Resurrection, and many others, all with life applications for daily living. Sunday school was the start of spiritual formation for the congregation, and assisted in navigating the obstacles of life." [109]

Kenneth H. Hill in *Religious Education in the African American Tradition* echoes this sentiment: Throughout the nineteenth century and into the twentieth century the Sunday school curriculum focused on integrating new converts into the Christian faith and life of the church. There was not a response within the Sunday curriculum to address racism, segregation, and racial discrimination. And examination of twentieth century Sunday school material reveals the neglect to address social justice issues and governments involvements in conflicts abroad. Instead the literature appeared to only be concerned with cultivating a personal devotion. However, as the Sunday school curriculum progressed it reveal a battle of good versus evil and through this perhaps some social justice issues could be construed"[110]

Sunday school served a dual purpose. Not only would these stories and discussions serve as a guide through life, but also as foundational knowledge for understanding the sermonic contexts of the preached word. The Sunday school education in the African American church was a family event, spanning several generations, all participating in learning the biblical narrative.

Religious education also prepared children for the public school setting. In the religious education setting, children learned how to sit, listen, respond, and communicate the things that were being taught. Religious education did not end when the worship service was over, but its content continued to live and was incorporated into daily activities. This could be seen and heard at the dinner table where Bible verses were recited by each family member seated at the table.

Religious education is responsible for shaping many lives in spiritual formations that extend far beyond the local congregation. This foundation would continue to shape believers of the love of Jesus Christ. Education has been the cornerstone in spiritual formation, parochial preparation and the shaping of the African American community and families. Although the community has changed, education is still a necessity for the neighborhood where the church has been called to join the missional plan of God.

The Cultural Shift

The 21st century brought with it a cultural shift in religious ideas and the family structure and values. Shows like Ozzie and Harriet, My Three Sons, Leave it to Beaver, and Father Knows Best, were no longer family prototypes. Although these particular shows depicted White suburban families, these were the only shows available to African American families. In some instance shows like the above mentioned were look at, as a lifestyle to attain, while others could find no way to identify and saw only the racial injustice perpetrated upon the Black community.

The African American church was no longer viewed by the majority as the center of community. Children are now deprived of the basic spiritual education, that was prominent in the African American Sunday school in the early 1960's. The African American family in the larger sense have now fallen away from faithful worship practices, and parents no longer send their children to learn and live out the biblical narrative. Although faith and family continued to be important values for the African American family, a large percentage of the people failed to incorporate those values in their daily lives. Instead they embraced new values such as assimilation, in order to seize that American dream. Independence was another value embraced, which allowed one to think that he or she could live independent of the larger urban community. The value of avariciousness, seeking only to gain wealth and possessions invaded the urban community, eventually allowing drug traffic, prostitution and increased violence."[111]

Shopkeepers now open their doors for business on Sundays and shopping malls of grandiose size have eroded communities as the ideology of a Sabbath faded into obscurity. Taverns no longer respected or reverenced God by closing their doors for the Sabbath. Their doors were open to receive patrons on the sacred day designed for worship. There are many reasons for the cultural shift, but the end result is that it has caused a disruption in family values.

This cultural shift not only deprived urban children of religious education, but also destroyed the worship practices and learning environments that held the family and community together.

Robert M. Franklin in *Crisis in The Village* conveys that the conditions that emerged out of the post-civil rights movements, caused community leaders to focus on legal battles, in this process they lost focus of the community itself, and failed to noticed that something was wrong from within."[112] This slow cultural shift drew attention and resources away from the centrality of the African American church, which was the base for religious education.

As CBF surveyed the community, it became apparent that the neighborhood was teaming with children. There was a common complaint that parents had no access to pre-school and limited access to full time kindergarten school for their children to attend. Around this same time in (August of 2010) due to budget constraints the city government revealed plans to reduce its Pre-K and Kindergarten class size in the public school system."[113] This action left many parents without access to public early childhood education.

It also forced some children, that should have been in formal and structured learning environments, to languish in child care services that may not have been developmentally appropriate.

During this period, public and private daycare sprang into action, gathering children in record numbers. They were able to complete high enrollment based on the government financial assistance known

as *CCIS* (Child Care Information Services). This government service provided funding for child care, but not for the education of
those same children. The child care centers were a great source for
babysitting services, but most neglected the spiritual care and lacked
the educational instruction needed to prepare them for the first year
of elementary school. Most entered into the public school system
at first grade level unable to recognized their names or letters of
the alphabet. These students matriculated through the educational
system, lacking the basic skills of reading, writing, and math.

Discouraged by what the congregation heard and saw, CBF
returned once again to prayer and fasting asking God how to respond
to the lost sheep. They inquired of God, how and where would they
join in God's missional plan. As they brainstormed about what
actions God was performing in the community, CBF re-evaluated
their resources and how they could be employed to bear the burden
of their neighbors.

Although a small urban congregation of about 35-40 members,
the CBF community consisted of public school teachers, firefighters,
police officers, nurses, dental assistants, UPS workers, hospital per-
sonnel, carpenters and factory workers. This make up in the CBF
congregation was not the norm for a small urban church, and particularly not the norm for the Kensington community. Some of the
leadership team held Bachelor and Master's degrees, which is also
an anomaly for a small urban church.

At CBF's disposal was the church and connecting building
complete with five classrooms, computer center, male and female
restrooms, kitchen facility and a huge multipurpose room for lunch
and physical activities. This church and connecting building was a
gracious gift from the previous congregation.

Obeying The Call to Educate

God had given the leadership team the vision to open a private, non-chartered, Christian Pre-K through 6th grade elementary
school. It was here that the CBF congregation believed that God was
active. This realization became evident as the congregation simply
opened its doors to help neighborhood children with their homework

assignments and school projects. It was informal, with just a few children stopping by for homework help. As the school year progressed more children began to join for homework help and the CBF church realized that they needed to formalized their help into an after school program.

During their first think tank, the leadership discussed what it would encompass to meet the legal requirement to have kids in the building during after school hours. Items that were addressed included: obtaining a Certificate of Occupancy issued by the Philadelphia Department of License and Inspections, seeking volunteers from within the congregation and community, securing criminal background checks and child abuse clearances, arranging for the provision of snacks, and distributing permission to parents authorizing their child to participate.

CBF further discussed requirements for participation, and decided every child must have some type of homework assignment. Security was also an issue to be reflected upon. Accomplishing the objectives provided in the think tanks took the entire summer. Getting appointments with city inspectors required patience and determination, there were long lines to wait in, many phone calls that went unreturned and appointments where inspectors never showed up. When the school year arrived, CBF was ready to officially launch its after school program. The after school program provided a safe haven from the streets until parents arrived at home. It was during this time; a deficiency was realized in the proficiency of the children's reading and comprehension skills.

A visit to the overcrowded classrooms of the nearby elementary school revealed why. One teacher was in charge of thirty or more students, some had matriculated without the basic skills for their grade level. There were some with clear behavioral issues, disrupting the class with outbursts and acts of violence.

Gretchin Lefever, Ph.D., of Eastern Virginia Medical School contends, that there is an over diagnosis of ADHD (Attention Deficit Hyper Activity Disorder) in children. In addition, 28 percent of the elementary school students who were medicated for ADHD in LeFever's study received two or more psychotropic drugs simultaneously. For many of them, treatment began during preschool or early childhood years."[114]

The school system private and public is caring for more and more children under the influenced of behavioral medications. Without spiritual care as well most children will be warehoused through the system."[115]

The leadership put together a standards-based reading comprehension program that would help them to comprehend the homework assignments given by the neighborhood school. During this year of operating the after school program, CBF again held think tank sessions surrounding the idea of creating a private Christian School own and operated by the house of worship. In those sessions, they discussed what operating a private Christian school would encompass. They first bathed the idea in prayer and decided to return with the team's pros and cons on the idea of instituting the private Christian school. As they reassembled two weeks later there were some team members that thought it might be too much for the congregation to handle, but the majority felt God's calling beyond the after school program. It was decided by the team to put it on hold for a year.

In May of 2010, while asleep God had awakened Pastor Mike at 2am and instructed him to start the elementary school the following September. Keep in mind that the school was not slated to open for another year. The message and voice of God was so clear, there was not a doubt that God was speaking to him. Pastor Mike awakened his wife and told her what the Lord had said to him. Lynne (his wife) agreed, quit her job and the process of preparing the school for opening began.

The think tank team discussed what they might possibly need to get started. The items discussed were: The costs of operation. CBF was in charge of a building that was empty six days out of the week and they were not exercising good stewardship with the facility that God had blessed them with. The congregation held no mortgage on the building, and only expenses they paid were utilities and insurance. Next they discussed how many teachers they would need to operate, and their salaries.

With limited resources, the school would have to rely on an all-volunteer staff. Including two teachers, two administrators and one food service assistant. A registered nurse from the congregation would volunteer on staff ten hours a week. Each volunteer would receive a monthly stipend as funds permitted.

As they continued their think tank sessions, the team realized they would need to hire an architect to draw up the floor plans for the City's Department of License and Inspection. Not only did they need architects but they needed electricians to bring building up to current fire codes. The team also understood that they needed to file documents with the Pennsylvania Departments of State and of Education.

Even though it was to be a Christian school, it should be registered as a "private, religious school." As a prerequisite and stepping stone to eventual accreditation. With this in mind the leadership team then focused on a name for the school. The name chosen would reflect their commitment to God and community. They chose Kensington Christian Academy as the name, hereafter known as KCA. With the formal logistics discussed, the team turn their attention to amending the church's bylaws, to include governance over the school.

While exploring the feasibility of providing such education to prospective students, the team weighed its options and constitutional rights to religiously educate its students. Although KCA was not accredited because they had not been in operation for five years according to the state guidelines, however they were registered with the state and was recognized by the state of Pennsylvania as a private religious school.

The team then developed the following mission statement: KCA's Mission is to: Provide an exceptional Pre-K- 6th grade education which boosts self-esteem, builds character, and equip students to engage their world in a purposeful way, by seamlessly integrating biblical principles and rigorous academics."[116]

The next matter to be attended was how instruction would be delivered at KCA. The best pedagogical approach to deliver rigorous instruction would be to utilize a standards-based curriculum which integrates biblical content." [117]

In an additional think tank session, at the suggestion of educational consultant, the team explored the implications of federal regulations such as: No Child Left Behind, PL 107-110, (NCLB, 2001); Individual Disability Education Act, (IDEA, 2004); and the Family

Education Rights and Privacy Act, (FERPA, 1974); and other policies and procedures that might impact KCA's student demographics. At this time the also designed internal policies and governing procedures." [118]

Faced with the task of getting the facility ready including school materials with only a budget of three thousand dollars, CBF sought how they could operate within that budget. Anthony G. Papas in *Inside The Small Church* writes "Another important aspect to creative thinking is the determination to use what we have. God has not called the small church to minister with what they do not have but with the resources placed at their disposal."[119] Re-evaluating their resources the congregation sought vender and donations from family and friends. As an independent church, CBF did not have a denomination affiliation, that they could turn to for support. Nor were they connected to any agencies that would assist them.

Carl S. Dudley in *Effective Small Churches: In the Twenty First Century* writes "Most small churches pay their own way. This is the secret of the majority of small congregations that have no denominational affiliation to appeal to, or no expectation of receiving funds to sustain them in a crisis. Money is not the problem. Independent and denominational small churches need imagination and determination more than financial support."[120] While it is true that imagination and determination must be the at the core of congregational thinking in the small church, but we must keep in mind that money plays an important role in congregational life.

This is especially true when a small church attempts to do ministry in urban communities that are lacking in basic resources. The neighborhood residents that have already been cast aside by the larger society, are seeking the churches assistance regardless of their size. They are truly looking to the small church for more than encouraging words.

In the epistle of James 2:15-16 NKJV, James writes to the believers encouraging them in their faith and works within the community. "If a brother or sister is naked and destitute of daily food, and one of you says to them, depart in peace, be warmed and filled, but does not give them the things which are needed for the body, what does it profit? The "missional sentness" of the small church must be coupled by word and deed. It is through these two that the small church embodies Christ. In (Acts 18:3, 20:34) the Apostle Paul made tents to sale. This tentmaking provided for his necessities and for those with him. This activity also allowed Paul to gain resources for sharing with the weak. The small church must have determination, imagination, resources, and most of all faith that God will provide all that is need for the missional work.

CBF began its process of opening the school with much prayer and relying totally in the resources on hand, and the power of God to sustain and create windows of opportunities. CBF knew that if God had gifted them this amazing church building, then he would also provide for the work of educating the children in the community. As the members of the congregation engaged the Department of License and Inspections, the Lord allowed them to meet a believer who was an architect. This architect's willingness to draft the city required building plans for a very modest fee, allowed KCA to hire other vendors.

Although they were working on a limited budget, the leadership team's faith in God would not allow that to become an obstacle. God was supernaturally sending provisions. Electricians were also needed to installed exit signs and lighting throughout the corridors. Once again the God of missions provided by sending electricians who grew up in the community and were willing to provide service at a rate affordable for KCA. As obstacles arose God's grace and mercy continued to provide avenues of blessings. These electricians performed the installation for a nominal fee. All of this was done on a budget of less than three thousand dollars. Everything was moving along and the church community was excited.

They were soon informed by the Department of Licenses and Inspections, that in order to be compliant with current ADA legislation, a ramp to allow handicap access must be constructed."[121] Here was another obstacle that KCA had not anticipated. Pastor Mike expressed this need to the architect who, on the church's behalf contacted builders who were associates of his, and shared with them the work that CBF was doing in the community. While the leadership team was praying for God to open a door, the construction company called and offered to build the entire handicap structure. They built it to the required city specifications, and also allowed the congregation to pay at their convenience. Truly God is active and the kingdom has come into the community. The faith of CBF was growing as God intervened in times of crisis.

With much prayer, anticipation and modest advertising the Kensington Christian Academy was poised to open its doors to the community. This would be the only private Christian school within the church's zip code. The school would serve several functions. Providing a great education and spiritual formation of the neighborhood children as well. The CBF congregation was blessed and excited how God was moving in the churches resources, bringing workers into their path to assist them just when things looked bleak. Little did leadership team realize, there would be continued obstacles in the missional plan of God.

Educational Obstacles

One of the concerns the leadership needed to address what kind of children they would accept to provide the best outcome? Brandon J. O'Brien in *The Strategically Small Church* warns us: When pastors function as commercial executives, they run the risk of viewing the congregation as consumers and patrons. This view can also easily attach itself to the community in which they are called to serve. It allows for the potential to lose focus of the churches mission, to join God in the redeeming work of Christ. The church will therefore be subject to the mindset of the secular business practices and that is to compete for its share of the market." [122]

The CBF congregation wanted to be cautious not to forget that they were on mission from Christ, and must keep that in the forefront of their minds. Distraction could now easily occur as the church shared it focus with budgets, applications and school fees. Not only was it a danger for the church in their view of the community, but also the community viewing the church as merchants of services and not displayers of grace.

Through the interview process it was determined that most of the Pre-K, Kindergarten and First grade children in the community were undeveloped educationally, and 95 % could not read, write or even recognize their name. It was KCA's belief that this was due to a lack of early childhood education in a formal setting. Most children in the community did not attend Pre-K, but rather, stayed home with the mother, grandmother and siblings.

This result of a lack of Pre-K echoed in SPECS: Scaling Progress in Early Childhood Settings is a core program of the Early Childhood Partnerships program (www.earlychildhoodpartnerships.org) of the University of Pittsburgh and affiliated with Children's Hospital of Pittsburgh." [123]

At age 4-6 most of the neighborhood children could not recognize letters of the alphabet and this was very disheartening to the education team at CBF. How could they possibly admit these students to a program designed to be academically rigorous? The staff at KCA thought that there was no possible way these children could begin to keep pace with the academic standards that would enable them to stand out from the public school system.

Then there were the issues of behavioral problems. Could KCA admit children with known behavioral issues and did they really want to? Many children had little to no home training or discipline. Some that applied to the school were children from single parent homes, and others from drug-addicted parents. These were children whose environments would not be productive for success. Franklin writes "The ancient Greek philosophers believed that ethical and philosophical instruction should began when children are young. In African culture, children were taught their identity and moral obligations within both the family household and in extended family/ village school." [124]

Without the church as the center of the community, promoting family values, and laying a foundation of spiritual formation through religious education, which began with the Sunday school, the urban community Pre-K and Kindergarten students entered the academic world at a deficit. How was CBF going to engage this community?

There were also children who had noticeable diminished mental capacities that did not fit within the paradigm of KCA's program of rigorist education. The leadership team was also faced with the task of considering the tuition fee, of a community that did not see the value in Christian education. Sustaining the cost of a private Christian school in a community dependent on public assistance would prove to be arduous at best. The magnitude of these obstacles were not fully realized by the leadership team of KCA.

KCA opened September of 2010, and soon the above mentioned issues began to overwhelmed the small urban church school, and the cost of operating the school became burdensome. One of the obstacles that KCA did not take into account was the energy required to operate a huge building 7 days a week. Prior to opening the school, the congregation was only in the church on Sundays for service and Wednesdays for Bible study. Now the school was using much more energy and the building was not energy friendly. Attendance was low. The CBF congregation funded the school's operation through its givers, and they began to feel the strain of operating the school. The leadership began to question if they were doing the right thing? Were they really doing what they were sent to do in the community? They held meetings to determine if they should keep the school open. This was not the position KCA and CBF thought they would find themselves. They re-evaluated the task and the role of education in the community, and came to the same conclusion, that this is where God had called them.

Three years went by without any real increase in students or support from the community. Enrollment was fluctuating and the neighborhood was in distress. There were still nagging and overwhelming questions such as: where was God? Had God abandoned them on the mission filed? Was it truly God's mission or the Pastor's mission? Pastor Mike and those under his leadership began to doubt God's activity in the community. Once again they went back to the think tanks. Praying and fasting trying to understand the community's response to the education of its children. CBF somehow needed to refocus and attach themselves to the work of God in the community.

Educational Refocusing

> Daniel Alexander Payne writes "Keep your children in
> the schools, even if you have to eat less, drink less and
> wear coarser raiment; though you eat but two meals a
> day; purchase but one change of garment during the

year, and relinquish all the luxuries of which we are
so fond, but which are as injurious to health and long
life as they are pleasing to the taste. Let the education
of your children penetrate the heart."[125]

KCA realized that before the community could value
education, the congregation had to value it themselves. The leadership team entered the community
placing the same monetary value on education like
most religious schools in the Philadelphia region and
across the country. Not only did KCA place a monetary value on education, but they also unknowingly
embraced a pull yourself up by your own bootstraps
mentality. The community had already been victim-
ized by deindustrialization, disinvestment and denied
social reform. A large percentage of its population
were addicted to drugs and alcohol. The CBF congregation expected them to function as redeemed sheep,
having experienced the resurrection power of the risen
Savior. This community did not have the discipline to
provide financially nor did they see a need of a spiritual education for their children. How could people
under such spiritual bondage deliver themselves?

It became apparent to the congregation, that families in the community were oppressed. This economic and systemic oppression
rendered them unable to give their children the identity needed to
function in society. It was the Black church's responsibility to shed
the light of the gospel into their dark world in order to foster that
identity, and break the cycle of poverty.

W.E.B. Du Bois writes "*The Talented Tenth*; the main question so far as the Southern Negro is concerned, is: What, under the
present circumstances, must a system of education do in order to
raise the Negro as quickly as possible in the scale of civilization?"[126]
The CBF congregation asked themselves that same question. What
must they do?

What must they do in the system of education in order to bring stability to the community? During the many think tank sessions, it was already established, that the focus would be on elementary age children, Pre-K through 6ᵗʰ grade. Reasons for this decision were as follows. First, the elementary age children were the fastest growing population in the community. this was determined as the leadership team inquired at local state representative office about the demographic of this population. Secondly, this cohort is the expressed image of God in the world for future generations. Third, they were still malleable even though some of them have been raised in tumultuous homes.

Franklin writes, "There is a growing industry concerned with teaching and promoting good character among elementary and secondary students. It is called the Character Education Movement."[127] In essence, this movement is aimed at teaching children what is right and wrong, developing character in everyday life situations.

It is through Christian education provided by the African American church, that character is developed and honed. Since the breakdown of the American family the church is no longer the primary molder of character formation, and the public school system is ill equip to perform the task. The new molders of character and consensus are rap videos, sport figures, gangsters, and satellite television. Therefore, the African American community has an increased number of recorded suspensions, expulsions and medications among elementary school children.

The Obama Administration focused on reducing the number of suspensions, expulsions and arrest in public schools, they also found a disturbing trend in 13 states. Blacks were suspended or expelled at rates higher than their representation in the schools. The reports show data for more ham 3,000 districts. The 13 states covered in the report are: Alabama, Arkansas, Florida, Georgia, Kentucky, Louisiana, Mississippi, North Carolina, South Carolina, Tennessee, Texas, Virginia, and West Virginia. Because of these suspensions and expulsions students will miss out on learning time, leading to eventual contact with the juvenile justice system."[128]

Listening to the voice of God is always difficult when He is saying things you might not want to hear. Submission of the leadership team was another key factor in the education process. KCA determined to abandon their will and way of thinking, and join God as the Holy Spirit worked in the community, however this part of the missional journey would come at a cost.

The Cost of Education

The KCA team somehow knew that they were on their own mission and had failed to join in God's mission. KCA was operating the school the way other Christian schools operated. Although they knew God had called them to start the school, they never sought how He wanted it accomplished.

After examining why student enrollment was declining, the KCA team began to evaluate the homes in which the students lived. As they examined the primary obstacle to education in the community, they saw a spiritual disconnection from God and deep spiritual poverty. It is not that the village did not care about education.

The KCA team realized the community did not see it as a priority in light of the essentials of everyday living expenses. A lifestyle oppressed by drugs, alcohol, and single or extended parenting, disabled the community to sacrifice for the educational benefit of their children. Under these conditions most residents, found it difficult to maintain their tuition obligations.

While examining the road to educating the children in this urban community they realized that the very building in which they worshipped and created a space for learning was a gift from God. The leadership team at KCA, finally understood that educating the community had to come without a price. It was the church's responsibility to ensure a sound religious and parochial education was made available. It was for this reason Christ has sent them. Finally, God's mission was revealed. The activity of God called for KCA to educate the community and trust God for the finances.

Let us keep in mind that the CBF congregation consisted at this time of 30-40 members. This is one of the things that made it all the more difficult to grasp God's mission. They were looking at their smallness and not God's greatness. They were operating out of their weakness and not in God's power. They were depending on their lack of resources and not God's Kingdom of abundance.

A Change in Educational Practices

In September 2014, KCA offered a totally free scholarship programs throughout the community. Parents that could pay were encouraged to do so, but those that could not were still received at the table of Christ. Students on scholarships were picked by lottery after being interviewed, and the parents/guardian will sign contracts to attend worship services weekly with their child, while volunteering 2 hours a week. This would ensure that the biblical values that are taught, were being reinforced through worship practices. It also provided an avenue of discipleship/support system for the parent/guardian. It is their hope that slowly the community will turn back to the African American church as its center for engaging all of life. Currently, KCA is believing, seeking, and connecting with those that the Master has called to come along side of them in God's mission. This small urban church continues to follow God into the trenches, as the story unfolds under the leadership of the Holy Spirit. They are sure to continue and experience God in new and wonderful ways as He supernaturally provides, sustains and gives victory to this small church.

Conclusion

The small church has many gifts and talents to offer the community in which it exists. These gifts can be fully realized when the small church operates out of the missional narrative of the Bible. The effectiveness of the small church depends on how willing they are to submit to mission of God as sent agents into communities. Whether urban, rural or suburban, God is truly active in small churches across the globe. Small urban churches can effect change in communities when they experience spiritual formation from within, as they embrace the *missio* Dei. Small urban churches are uniquely tasked to live out the kingdom agenda among the disinherited and disenfranchised. It is the author's fervent prayer that small and large churches connect with each other, to strengthen, encourage and spur one another to continue good works. The small church is not independent of the large church and vice versa. Each is called to live out the transformative power of the gospel in the communities in which they are sent. When the small church internalized its sentness to join God in mission, it is then it will recognize its greatness in the greatness of Jesus Christ. To small churches across the globe urban, rural, suburban, stay the course, trust in God for everything and above all don't give up!

Glossary

ADA: The Americans with Disabilities Act (ADA) prohibits discrimination against people with disabilities in employment, transportation, public accommodation, communications, and governmental activities.

ADHD: Attention deficit hyperactivity disorder: A disorder in which a person is unable to control behavior due to difficulty in processing neural stimuli, accompanied by an extremely high level of motor activity.

AFDC: Aid to Dependent Families- AFDC (Aid to Families with Dependent Children) is a program administered and funded by Federal and State governments to provide financial assistance to needy families.

Bivocational or Tentmaker: A pastor or clergy who works a secular job outside of their ministerial duties within the congregation. This allowed pastors and clergy to help support the church financially.

CBF: The Christ Bible Fellowship Church: A non-denominational church founded and located in Philadelphia, Pennsylvania. This church practices a reformed theology with belief in a Trinitarian God. Its primary focus is to live out the transforming power of the gospel in community, while joining God in mission through life together in community.

CCIS: The Subsidized Child Day Care Program offers low-income parents assistance to pay for child care. Child Care Information Services (CCIS) are independent agencies contracted by the Department of Public Welfare to authorize day care through local providers.

Christotelic: New Testament Theology affirms that a Christotelic hermeneutic is an essential to correctly interpret Scripture. Explanation of the biblical text which does not consistently employ the aforementioned hermeneutic will result in a less accurate interpretation of God's Word. A Christotelic hermeneutic views the Lord Jesus Christ as the ultimate goal or end of God's Word and seeks to consistently interpret all Scripture in view of this great truth. Michael Kelly, 'Biblical Theology and Missional Hermeneutics: A Match Made *for* Heaven... on Earth? 'in P. Enns, and D.J. Green Eyes *to See, Ears to Hear: Essays in Memory of J. Alan Groves* (Phillipsburg: P&R Publishing, 2010), 61-76.

City of Brotherly Love: The name Philadelphia means "the city of brotherly love" in Greek. It was named by its founder, William Penn, who envisioned a city of religious tolerance where no one would be persecuted. He also hoped to live at peace with the native Americans and paid them fairly for the rights to the city's land.

Deindustrialization: Deindustrialization refers to the process of social and economic change ignited by the removal or reduction of industrial activity. Deindustrialization can have serious socioeconomic consequences in urban areas that used to be reliant on the manufacturing industry for jobs.

Drug Traffic: Is a global illicit trade involving the distribution and sale of substances which are subject to drug prohibition laws.

Eikons: Humans representing God in the world. They are earth's divine representatives. Eikons are humans that reveal the image of God in relationship with God and other Eikons and the world.

Eikons are God-oriented, self-oriented, and other-oriented and cosmos-oriented.

FERPA: The Family Educational Rights and Privacy Act (FERPA) (20 U.S.C. § 1232g; 34 CFR Part 99) is a Federal law that protects the privacy of student education records. The law applies to all schools that receive funds under an applicable program of the U.S. Department of Education. FERPA gives parents certain rights with respect to their children's education records.

House Church: House church or home church is a label used to describe an independent assembly of Christians who gather for worship in a home. Sometimes these groups meet because the membership is small, and a home is the most appropriate place to gather, as in the beginning phase of the British New Church Movement.

Hyper- Individualism: Creating a personal relationship with God, exclusive of need for communal worship or congregation interaction.

IDEA: The Individuals with Disabilities Education Act (IDEA) is a law ensuring services to children with disabilities throughout the nation. IDEA governs how states and public agencies provide early intervention, special education and related services to more than 6.5 million eligible infants, toddlers, children and youth with disabilities.

ISLAM: Muslims call their religion Islam, and the Arabic word Islam implies the attainment of peace through submission to Allah. The word Muslim is an adjective derived from the noun Islam, and implies one who has peace within himself from his submission to Allah. Muslims believe in the One, Eternal God, who created the heavens and the earth and all that exists.

KCA: KCA stands for The Kensington Christian Academy. A private Christian school owned and operated by the Christ Bible Fellowship Church. It provides an exceptional Pre-K- 6th grade education which boosts self-esteem, builds character, and equips students to engage their world in a purposeful way, by seamlessly integrating biblical principles and rigorous academics.

Mega Church: The term mega-church generally refers to any Protestant Christian congregation with a sustained average weekly attendance of 2,000 persons or more in its worship services, counting all adults and children at all its worship locations. Mega churches host a multitude of social, recreational, and aid ministries.

Missio Dei: Newbigin's interpretation of the *missio* Dei aims to give an explanation of how God is the missionary and, secondarily, of the way in which God's mission involves the church. The mission is indeed God's in the sense, God's kingdom dawns as the Father sends the Son into the world to redeem it from sin. When the Son ascends to the right hand of the Father, the Son also sends the apostles into the world to continue the saving mission in the power of the Holy Spirit. God initiated this mission, and also upholds its current work, and will bring it to consummation.

Missions/Missional: It is an understanding that the mission belongs to God. The church understands that in any place it is a community sent by God. "Mission" is not something the church does, as part of its total program. No, the church's essence is missional, for the calling and sending action of God forms its identity. Mission is founded on the mission of God in the world, rather than the church's effort to extend itself.

NBA: National Basketball Association.

NCAA: National Collegiate Athletic Association.

NFL: National Football League.

Renewal: A renewal of the people's ability to notice and experience God in their midst, a renewal of the congregation's desire to partner with God in achieving God's aims for the world. What is renewed in congregational renewal is the peoples understanding of their relationship with God, their relationship with their community, and their sense of calling.

SPECS: Scaling Progress in Early Childhood Settings is a core program of the Early Childhood Partnerships program of the University of Pittsburgh and affiliated with Children's Hospital of Pittsburgh SPECS uses an Authentic Assessment approach, which is required by national professional organizations for use in the field and is part of quality professional standards by the National Association for the Education of Young Children.

Spiritual formation: Spiritual formation is the process of apparent spiritual development through engaging in a set of behaviors, termed disciplines. Advocates believe these disciplines help shape the character of the practitioner into the likeness of Christ. Spiritual formation is a process, but it is also a journey through which we open our hearts to a deeper connection with God.

Storefront Church: The storefront church phenomenon is familiar to historically Black American communities. In these Black American communities an old store that is not in use is bought or rented and used as a place to hold religious services serving the needs of the community. Storefront and community churches have remained strong influences in Black America, offering educational and financial resources in addition to religious ministry.

End Notes

Chapter One: Biblical and Theological Foundations of Small Church Ministry

1   Lyle E. Schaller, *Small Congregation Big Potential* (Nashville, TN: Abington Press,2003), 25.

2   Lyle E. Schaller, *The Small Church is Different* (Nashville, TN: Abington Press,1982), 11.

3   Feeney, Jim. "Small Churches Please God, Too. Sermons on The Church."
Available from: http://www.jimfeeney.org/small-churches.html. (accessed September 18, 2014).

4   Ibid.1-4.

5   Ibid:1-4.

6   Barbero, Mario. *A First-Century Couple, Priscilla and Aquila: Their House Churches and Missionary Activity*.2001. Available from: http://fulfillment.umi.com/dissertations/d3d6e-c04088e966785bf3b44265684cb/1444939120/3004148.pdf

7   Giles, Kevin. *House Churches*. Winter, Vol.24, No.1. 2010. Available from www.cbeinternational.org/sites/default/files/house_Giles.pdf_(accessed November 2015).

8   Brandon J. O'Brien, *The Strategically Small Church* (Bloomington, MN: Bethany House Publishers,2010), 29.

9   Anthony G. Pappas, *Inside The Small Church* (Herndon, VA: Alban Institute Publishers, 2002), 2.

10   Ibid.;2.

11 Ibid.;3.

12 David R. Ray, *The Big Small Church Book* (Cleveland OH: The Pilgrim Press, 1992), vii.

13 May, Douglas, C. Why Are There Small Churches? Concordia Theological Quarterly Vol 67:1(January 2003):87 www.ctsfw. net/media/pdfs/CTQTheologicalobserver67-1pfd. [accessed April 02,2015].

14 Ibid.; 87.

15 Katie Day, *Faith on the Avenue*, (New York, NY: Oxford University Press, 2014), 23.

16 Mantone, Amanda.2004. "Storefront Churches Are Lifeblood to Urban Poor." The Christian Century, Vol 121, Issue 8. http://www.questia.com/read/1G1-115833952/store-front-churches-are-lifeblood-to-urban-poor (accessed April 8,2015).

17 Katie Day, *Faith on the Avenue*, (New York, NY: Oxford University Press, 2014), 112.

18 Mantone, Amanda. *Storefront Churches Are Lifeblood to Urban Poor.* The Christian Century, Vol 121, Issue 8.2004. Available from: http://www.questia.com/read/1G1-115833952/storefront-churches-are-lifeblood-to-urban-poor (accessed April 8,2015).

19 The Baptist Union of Great Britain, "Small Churches Project." Report to Council. March 2005. Available from http://easternbaptist.org.uk/files/smallchurchBU.pdf (accessed May 14, 2015).

20 By the mid-century, the emphasis in mission thought shifted toward a *theocentric* approach that, in contrast stressed the mission of God (missio Dei) as the foundation for the mission of the church. The church became redefined as the community spawned by the mission of God and gathered up into that mission. The church was coming to understand that in any place it is a community sent by God. "Mission" is not something the church does, a part of its total program. No, the church's essence is missional, for the calling and sending action of God forms its identity. Mission is founded on the mission of God in the world, rather than the church's effort to

extend itself. Darrel L. Guder, Missional Church: A Vison for the sending of the church in North America (Grand, Rapids, MI: Eerdmans Publishing,1998),81-82.

21 The Baptist Union of Great Britain, "Small Churches Project." Report to Council. March 2005. Available from http:// easternbaptist.org.uk/files/smallchurchBU.pdf (accessed May14, 2015).

22 Anthony G. Pappas, *Anthony, Inside The Small Church* (Herndon, VA: Alban Institute Publishers, 2002), 3-4.

23 Carl S. Dudley, *Effective Small Churches in the Twenty –first Century*, (Nashville TN: Abington Press, 2003), 25.

24 Ibid.; 25.

25 Carl S. Dudley, *Effective Small Churches in the Twenty –first Century*, (Nashville TN: Abington Press, 2003), 25.

26 Ibid.; 20.

27 David R. Ray, *The Big Small Church Book* (Cleveland OH: The Pilgrim Press, 1992), 1.

28 Anthony G. Pappas, *Anthony, Inside The Small Church* (Herndon, VA: Alban Institute Publishers, 2002), 132-133.

29 Perter Bush, and Christine O'Reilly, *Where 20 or 30 Are Gathered: Leading Worship in the Small Church* (Herndon, VA: Alban Institute Publishers, 2006), 23-24.

30 Carl S. Dudley, *Effective Small Churches in the Twenty –first Century*, (Nashville TN: Abington Press, 2003), 183. 1.This model of the independent, self-sufficient ministry has biblical foundations in the ministry of the apostle Paul (Acts 18:3, 20:34). It has always been strong in independent churches, whose affirmation of the transforming work of the Holy Spirit has an anti-intellectual aspect. Tentmaking was more than an alternative means of financial support. It provided pastors with direct, personal, and continuous contact with the work-world reality of parishioners. 2.The contemporary tentmaker come from all sorts of backgrounds, labor and management, farmers and teachers, factory workers and social counselors. By any standard, bivocational clergy as a group have spent more years in higher education and hold more advanced degrees than comparable clergy who have a single calling.

On the whole, they are remarkably gifted group of pastors, most of whom felt underemployed with a single vocation.

31 Carl S. Dudley, *Effective Small Churches in the Twenty –first Century*, (Nashville TN: Abington Press, 2003), 183.

32 Lyle E. Schaller, *The Small Church is Different*, (Nashville TN: Abington Press, 1982), 94.

33 Ibid.; 94.

Chapter Two: Small Beginnings / a Personal Ministry Experience

34 Katie Day, *Faith on the Avenue: Religion on a City Street* (New York, NY: Oxford Press, 2014),1, 43. 1.Germantown Avenue has been something between a project and an obsession. The Revolutionary battle was fought on this street. Stone buildings where British troops were billeted still stand. George Washington and Thomas Jefferson escaped the epidemic by moving out of Center City into the stalely homes that still grace the avenue. Over a century before, in 1688, the first remonstrance against slavery was lodged by members of the Germantown Avenue Mennonite Quaker congregation. 2. Entering the old furniture factory, Muslim worshippers quietly slip out of their shoes before finding a space on the prayer carpet. Not far up the Avenue, Mennonites silence their animated greetings as they entered the renovated iron works warehouse and retailer, and transition into private meditation in preparation for worship. A few blocks away, the simple altar in the shoe store, adorned with plastic flowers around the wooden cross reverence the majestic Basilica. Pentecostal worshippers whisper, and then shout, their adoration of God. On this one city street, ordinary space becomes holy ground.

35 Hibbert, Richard Y. "The place of church planting in mission: Towards a theological Framework." '*Evangelical Review of Theology*, ERT (2009): 33(4): 316-331.

36 Thomas J. Surge, *Origins of the Urban Crisis, Race and inequality in Postwar Detroit*. (Princeton, NJ: Princeton University Press,1996), xxxix University Press,1996), xxxix.

37   Ron Daniels. *"Reasserting the Vision/Mission of Black Nationalism: Remembering Malcolm in a Time of Crisis."* Institute of The Black World. Available from http://ibw21.org/vantage-pont/reasserting-the-visionmission-of-black-nationalism-remembering-malcom-in-a-time-of-crisis (accessed July2015).

38   David. R. Ray, *The Big Small Church Book,* (Cleveland Ohio: The Pilgrim Press, 1992), 190-191 1. "Rural America's most recent dramatic problem was the farm crisis of the mid 1980s, when over 500,000 American farms failed. When the crash came, many farmers couldn't pay back their loans. Many had to quit farming, farms were sold or foreclosed on, farm families migrated elsewhere in search of employment, farm-related business and industry suffered, and communities were devastated. The loss of population and tax base results in loss of services and the consolidation of schools. The fruits of the crisis were and are severe emotional stress, suicide, family dysfunction and breakup, unemployment, community distress and despair, and church decline.

39   In Kensington, more than 40% of home owners are cost-burdened, and that proportion jumps to nearly two-thirds of all Kensington renters. Kensington has almost double the percentage of renters living in subsidized housing, as well. During the early 20th century, the greater Kensington area contained a booming manufacturing industry. Beginning in the 1950s, however, deindustrialization swept through Philadelphia. Warehouses began to close, and many Kensingtonians lost their jobs. According to the Philadelphia Daily News, between 1979 and 1983, almost thirty years after deindustrialization roughly began, Philadelphia lost 100,000 jobs, many of which were in the Kensington neighborhood (Eisberg). The picture in Kensington and East Kensington bleak. Unemployment is high. People are working in jobs with little to no upward mobility and low salaries Available from: https://kensington-philadelphia.wordpress.com/ (accessed February 2016).

40 John M. Perkins, Beyond Charity: *The Call to Christian Community Development* (Grand Rapids, MI: Baker Books Publishers, 1993), 26.

41 Jacobson, Rolf, A. "The Lord is God of Justice" (Isaiah 30:18): *The Prophetic Insistence on Justice in Social Context"* Word & World Volume 30, No.2, (Spring 2010):125.

1.The Lord is a God of Justice; The Prophetic Insistence on Justice in Social Context" writes "Justice is a social concept. It has to do with the order of society and how that order shapes or fails to shape human relationship with one another. A society that is "more just" is one in which the social order allows life to thrive to a greater degree. A society that is "less just" is one in which the social order prevents life from thriving to a greater degree.

42 New Covenant Theology affirms that a *Christotelic* hermeneutic is an essential tool to correctly interpret Scripture. Explanation of the biblical text which does not *consistently* employ the aforementioned hermeneutic will result in a less accurate interpretation of God's Word. *A Christotelic hermeneutic views the Lord Jesus Christ as the ultimate goal or end of God's Word and seeks to consistently interpret all Scripture in view of this great truth.* Furthermore, this particular method of interpretation emphasizes five principles: 1) the person and work of the Lord Jesus Christ is *the nexus* of God's plan in redemptive history; 2) *all* Scripture either refers to Christ *directly* (e.g. the Gospel narratives, messianic prophecies), or refers to Christ *typologically*, or *prepares the way* for Christ by unfolding redemptive history which ultimately points to His person and work (e.g. the Flood, the calling of Abraham); 3) *the New Testament Scriptures must have interpretive priority over the Old Testament (OT)*; 4) an accurate analysis of a passages context (i.e. local, literary, Scriptural, and historical) is key; and 5) the principle of historical-grammatical interpretation (guided by principles 1-4). Peter Enns writes: A Christotelic approach is an attempt to look at the centrality of Christ for hermeneutics in a slightly different way. It asks not so much, how does this OT passage, episode, figure, etc.,

lead to Christ? To read the OT Christotelicly is to read it already knowing that Christ is somehow the end (telos) to which the OT story is heading; in other words, to read the OT in light of the exclamation point of the history of revelation, the death and resurrection of Christ. Available from: http://nct-blog.ptsco.org/2012/09/03/christotelic-hermeneutics-part-1/ (accessed February 2016).

43 Mott, Stephen, Slider, Ronald, J. "Economic Justice: biblical paradigm" *Transformation* (April 2000): 50.

44 Ibid.;50.

45 Allen J Roxburgh and Fred Romanuk, *"The Missional Leader"* (San Francisco, CA: Jossey-Bass, 2006),9.

46 Daniel P. Smith, Mary K. Sellon, *Pathways to Renewal* (Herndon, VA: The Alban Institute, 2008), 7.

Chapter Three: A Need for Spiritual Formation

47 Daniel P. Smith. Mary K. Sellon, *Pathways to Renewal*, (Herndon, VA: Alban Institute, 2008), 7-8. 1.When we talk about congregational renewal, we mean a renewal of the people's ability to notice and experience God in their midst, a renewal of the congregation's desire to partner with God in achieving God's aims for the world. What's renewed in congregational renewal is the peoples understanding of their relationship with God, their relationship with their community, and their sense of calling.

48 John P. Kotter. *Leading Change*: (Washington, DC: Library of Congress, 2012), 38.

49 Juan C. Ortiz, *Call To Discipleship*, (Plainfield, NJ: Logos International, 1975), 99.

50 Dietrich, Bonhoeffer, *The Cost of Discipleship,* (New York, NY: Touch Press, 1995), 43.

51 Ibid.;44-45.

52 Ibid.;62.

53 Ibid.; 59.

54 Christin Research Network: Spiritual formation is the process of apparent spiritual development through engaging in a

set of behaviors, termed disciplines. Advocates believe these disciplines help shape the character of the practitioner into the likeness of Christ. Though superficially similar to discipleship, spiritual formation is not merely concerned with biblical exhortation and instruction in orthodox doctrine, but also with the teaching of "many practices that opened the believer to the presence and direction of God, and nurtured the character traits of Christ into fruition." Spiritual formation is a process, but it is also a journey through which we open our hearts to a deeper connection with God. We are not bystanders in our spiritual lives, we are active participants with God, who is ever inviting us into relationship with him. Available from: http://christianresearchnetwork.org/topic/spiritual-formation/ (access February 2016).

55 Ibid.; 43.

56 Edward N. Gross, *Are You a Christian or a Disciple?* United States of America: Xulon Press, 2014, 64.

57 Ibid.; 180.

58 Juan C. Ortiz, Disciple: *A Handbook for New Believers*, (Lake Mary, FL: Creation House), 1995.

59 John Coe, "Resisting The Temptation Of Moral Formation: Opening To Spiritual Formation In The Cross And The Spirit." Vol.1, No. 1 (2008): 54-78.

60 Willard, Dallas, "Spiritual Formation And The Warfare Between The Flesh And The Human Spirit" Journal of Spiritual Formation & Soul Care (2013): 152.

61 John F. Walvoord, Roy B. Zuck, *The Bible Knowledge Commentary: New Testament Edition*, (Eastbourne, England: Chariot Victor Publishing, 1983), 321-322.

62 Stephen Hong, "*Reversing A Downward Spiral: Strengthening The Church's Community, Holiness and Unity Through Intentional Discipleship*," Asian Journal of Pentecostal Studies 15:1 (2012): 92.

63 Glenn C. Daman, *Shepherding the Small Church* (Grand Rapids, MI: Kregel Publications, 2008), 122.

64 Simon Schrock, *One Anothering*, (Green Forest, AR: New Leaf Press, 1991),120.

65   Peter K. Nelson, "Discipleship Dissonance: Toward A Theology of Imperfection Amidst the Pursuit of Holiness" *Journal of Spiritual Formation & Soul Care*, VOL.4, No 1, (2011): 63-92.

Chapter Four: Small Church / Missional Church

66   MacIlvaine III, Rodman W. "What Is The Missional Church Movement?" *Bibliotheca Sacra 167* (January -March 2010):89-106.

67   1.Allen J Roxburgh and Fred Romanuk, *"The Missional Leader"* (San Francisco, CA: Jossey-Bass).

2. Reggie McNeal, *Missional Renaissance* (San Francisco, CA: Jossey-Bass Publishers, 2009).

3. Rick Rouse and Craig Van Gelder, *A Filed Guide for The Missional Congregation* (Minneapolis, MN: Augsburg Fortress Press, 2008).

4. Eddie Gibbs, *Church Next* (Madison, WI: Intervarsity Press, 2000).

68   Darrell L. Guder, *Missional Church, A Vision for the Sending of the Church in North America* (Grand Rapids, MI: Wm. B. Eerdmans Publishing Co., 1998), 4.

69   Ibid.; 4.

70   W. Rodman MacIlvaine III, "What Is The Missional Church Movement?" *Bibliotheca Sacra 167* (January -March 2010):89-106.

71   Darren Sarisky, "The Meaning of the missio Dei: Reflections on Lesslie Newbigin's Proposal That Mission Is of the Essence of the Church" Missiology: An International Review, Vol 42(3) (2014): 257-270.

1.Newbigin's interpretation of the *missio* Dei aims to give an explanation of how God is the missionary and, secondarily, of the way in which God's mission involves the church. The mission is indeed God's in the sense, God's kingdom dawns as the Father sends the Son into the world to redeem it from sin. When the Son ascends to the right hand of the Father, he sends the apostles into the world to continue his saving mission in the power of His Spirit. God initiated this mission, he upholds its current work, and will bring it to consummation.

72 W. Rodman MacIlvaine III, "What Is The Missional Church Movement?" Bibliotheca Sacra 167 (January -March 2010): 91.

73 Reggie McNeal, *Missional Renaissance* (San Francisco, CA: Jossey-Bass, 2009), 20, 21.

74 Rick Rouse and Craig Van Gelder, *A Field Guide For The Missional Congregation* (Minneapolis, MN: Augsburg Fortress Press, 2008), 48,49.

75 Eleanor Scott Meyers, *Envisioning The New City* (Louisville, Kentucky: John Knox Press, 1992), 146.

76 W. Rodman MacIlvaine III, "What Is The Missional Church Movement?" *Bibliotheca Sacra 167* (January -March 2010):89-106.

77 Ibid.; 89-106.

78 Eleanor Scott Meyers, *Envisioning The New City* (Louisville, Kentucky: John Knox Press, 1992),101.

79 Jim Kitchens, "The *Postmodern Parish: New Ministry for a New Era* (Bethesda, MI: Alban Institute, 2003), 75.

80 W. Rodman MacIlvaine III, "What Is The Missional Church Movement?" *Bibliotheca Sacra 167* (January -March 2010):104.

81 Ibid.; 104-106.

82 Scot McKnight, *The Jesus Creed* (Brewster, MA: Paraclete Press, 2004).

83 Ibid.; 8.

84 Scot McKnight, *The Jesus Creed* (Brewster, MA: Paraclete Press, 2004),13.

85 Ibid.; 35.

86 Ibid.; 36.

87 Ibid.; 39.

88 Scott McKnight, *A Community Call Atonement* (Nashville, TN: Abington Press, 2007), 9.

89 Reggie McNeal, *Missional Renaissance* (San Francisco, CA: Jossey-Bass, 2009), 134, 135.

90 Ridderbos, The Coming of the Kingdom, trans. H. de Jongste (Philadelphia: The Presbyterian and Reformed Publishing Company, 1976), 354.
91 Alan J. Roxburgh, *Missional: Joining God in The Neighborhood* (Grand Rapids, MI: Baker Books Publishing, 2011), 150.
92 Scott McKnight, *A Community Call Atonement* (Nashville, TN: Abington Press, 2007), 11.
93 Joel R.E. Hunt, *Thy Kingdom Come* (Augustana Book Concern, 1920), 13,14.
94 Gordon C. Lund, *Thy Kingdom Come* (Philadelphia, PA: Muhlenberg Press, 1958), 127-130.
95 Craig W. Ellison, *The Urban Mission* (Grand Rapids, MI: William B. Eerdmans Pub. Co, 1974), 15.
96 Scott McKnight, *A Community Call Atonement* (Nashville, TN: Abington Press, 2007), 15-21.

Chapter Five: Connecting To Community

97 Diana Bass, Grounded: Finding God In The World, A Spiritual Revolution (New York, NY: Harper Collins Publishers, 2015), 196.
98 Walter Kloetzli and Arthur Hillman, *Urban Church Planning* (Philadelphia, PA: Muhlenberg Press, 1958), 25.
99 Diana Bass, *Grounded: Finding God In The World, A Spiritual Revolution* (New York, NY: Harper Collins Publishers, 2015), 196.
100 Ibid.; 196-197.
101 Scot McKnight, *The Jesus Creed* (Brewster, MA: Paraclete Press, 2004), 117.
102 Stephen C. Rasor and Christine D. Chapman, *Black Power From The Pew: Laity Connecting Congregations and Communities* (Cleveland, Ohio: The Pilgrim Press, 2007), 23-24.
103 Edward P. Wimberley, *African American Pastoral Care* (Nashville TN: Abingdon Press, 2008), 13.
104 Ibid.; 20.

105 Ibid.; 128.

Chapter Six: Rebuilding Community Through Education

106 Probability of competing in sports beyond high school: Available from: http://www.ncaa.org/about/resources/research/probability-competing-beyond-high-school (Accessed January 2016) This information was provided by the (NCAA) National Collegiate Athletic Association in the United States. The National Collegiate Athletic Association is a member -led organization dedicated to the well-being and lifelong success of college athletes. The NCAA is committed to enforcing the rules, creating fair competition and establishing a positive competitive environment for student – athletes across the country. It's the responsibility of the universities, athletics programs, coaches, alumni, student- athletes and national office staff to be fully accountable at every level. All statistics reported to the NCAA should be compiled by the host institution press box/row statistics staff during the contest. Any exceptions to these guidelines must clearly be documented with rationale provided, explaining why in-contest statistics were not available.

107 Probability of competing in sports beyond high school: Available from: http://www.ncaa.org/about/resources/research/probability-competing-beyond-high-school (Accessed January 2016).

108 Braunfeld v. Brown (1961): Available from: http://atheism.about.com/library/decisions/holydays/bldec_BraunfeldBrown.htm (accessed February 2016).

109 For a historical background in Sunday Schools See. http://www.encyclopedia.com/topic/Sunday_school.aspx (accessed February 2016).

110 Kenneth H. Hill, *Religious Education in The African American Tradition* (Danvers, MA, Chalice Press, 2007),19-23.

111 Robert M. Franklin, *Crisis In The Village: Restoring Hope in African American Communities* (Minneapolis, MN: Fortress Press, 2007), 17-18.

112 "Robert M. Franklin, Crisis In The Village: Restoring Hope in African American Communities (Minneapolis, MN: Fortress Press, 2007), 17.

113 "The Philadelphia School District's plan to cut full-day kindergarten to help balance its budget is being decried by national education experts as a "disaster" and a "very bad decision" that could harm the development of thousands of children–especially the poor. At the same time, many Philadelphia parents are angered and worried that half-day kindergarten would force them to choose between quitting work to be home for their children or placing them in questionable or costly day care. And local child advocates warn that community child-care centers could not handle the tidal wave of 12,700 kindergartners likely to need placement in some kind of program. If we don't give kids a chance, there's no hope for a future–theirs or ours." Available from: http://articles.philly.com/2011-05-01/news/29493380_1_full-day-kindergarten-half-day-kindergarten-block-grant. (accessed February 2016).

114 Medicating ADHD: Too much? Too Soon? Available from: http://www.apa.org/monitor/dec01/medicating.aspx (Accessed January 2016).

115 Ibid.;1.

116 KCA's Mission: Providing an exceptional PreK-6th grade education which boosts self-esteem, builds character, and equips students to engage their world in a purposeful way, by seamlessly integrating biblical principles and rigorous academics. Bully-free learning environment. Instruction based on state & national standards. Promotes sense of family and community. Competitive tuition structure Our Curriculum ... In preparing students for meaningful participation in an increasingly diverse and global world, KCA offers individualized standards-based instruction designed to build and sustain proficiency in reading, language arts, math, science, and social studies." Available from: http://www.christbiblefellowshipministries.com/pages.asp?pageid=91810 (accessed February 2016).

117 "Christian schools come in all shapes and sizes. Some are one-room schoolhouses which make use of self-paced curriculum packets; others are structured in much the same manner as public schools. Some are either affiliated with or part of a church or are independent. Common to all schools, however, is a strict adherence to an established interpretation of fundamentalist religious and social values. The curriculum method utilized by Christian educators often varies considerably from school to school." Neal Devin's, "State Regulation of Christian Schools" (1983). *Faculty Publications*. Paper 381. Available from: http://scholarship.law.wm.edu/facpubs/381 (accessed February 2016).

118 For more information on educational legislation see the below link. Available from: http://www2.ed.gov/policy/landing.jhtml (accessed February 2016).

119 Anthony G. Pappas, *Inside The Small Church* (Washington, DC: Alban Institute,2002), 137.

120 Carl S. Dudley, *Effective Small Churches in the Twenty-First Century* (Bethesda, Maryland: Abingdon Press, 2003), 181-183.

121 Adoption of the 2010 Standards also establishes a revised reference point for Title II entities that choose to make structural changes to existing facilities to meet their program accessibility requirements; and it establishes a similar reference for Title III entities undertaking readily achievable barrier removal.

Available from: http://www.ada.gov/regs2010/2010ADAStandards/2010ADAstandards.htm#pgfId-1006877 (accessed February 2016).

122 Brandon J. O'Brien, *The Strategically Small Church* (Bloomington, Minnesota: Bethany House Publishers, 2010), 82-83.

123   "Early Childhood Partnerships: 10,000 high-risk and ulnerable preschool children showed significant gains in development and early learning skills in spoken language, reading, writing, math, classroom behavior, and daily living skills toward average (age-expected). Actual developmental

progress rates after participation in PKC exceeded children's" expected maturational rates before participation in PKC. Developmental progress rates in some skill areas exceeded the statistical indices established in national early childhood intervention studies. Preschoolers with longest PKC participation—until transition to kindergarten—showed the strongest gains in early learning skills." Available from: http://www.heinz.org/userfiles/library/execsum-final.pdf (accessed February 2016).

124 Robert M. Franklin, *Crisis In The Village: Restoring Hope in African American Communities* (Minneapolis, MN: Fortress Press, 2007), 203-204.

125 Robert M., Franklin, *Crisis In The Village* (Minneapolis, MN: Augsburg, Fortress, 2007), 181-182.

126 Ibid.; 197.

127 Ibid.; 205.

128 Analysis Finds Higher Expulsion Rates for Black Students. Available from: http://www.nytimes.com/2015/08/25/us/higher-expulsion-rates-for-blacks-students-are-found.html?_r=0

Selected Bibliography

Barbero, Mario. "A First Century Couple, Priscilla and Aquila: Their House Churches and Missionary Activity. Available from http://fulfillment.umi.com/dissertations/d3d6ec04088e966785bf3b44265684cb/1444939120/3004148.pfd (accessed September 18, 2014).

Bass, Diana, *Grounded: Finding God In The World, A Spiritual Revolution,* New York, NY: Harper Collins Publishers, 2015.

Black Students Expulsion: Available from: http://www.nytimes.com/2015/08/25/us/higher-expulsion-rates-for-blacks-students-are-found.html?=0 (accessed February 2016).

Bonhoeffer, Dietrich. *The Cost of Discipleship*, New York, NY: Touch Press, 1995.

Braunfeld v. Brown (1961): Jacob Braunfeld. Available from: http://atheism.about.com/library/decisions/holydays/bldec-Braunfeld-Brown.htm (accessed February 2016).

Bush, Peter and O'Riley Christine. *Where 20 or 30 Are Gathered: Leading Worship in the Small Church.* Herndon, VA: Alban Publishers, 2006.

Christian Research Network: Research Spiritual Formation. Available from http://christianresearchnetwork.org/topic/spiritual-formation/ (accessed February 6, 2016).

Christian Schools: Available from: http://scholarship.law.wm.edu/facpubs/381 (accessed February 2016).

Coe, John "Resisting The Temptation Of Moral Formation: Opening To Spiritual Formation In The Cross And The Spirit." *Vol.1*, No. 1 (2008): 54-78.

Dallas, Willard. "Spiritual Formation And The Warfare Between The Flesh And The Human Spirit" Journal of Spiritual Formation & Soul Care (2013): 152

Daman, Glenn C. *Shepherding the Small Church*. Grand Rapids, MI: Kregel Publications, 2008.

Daniels, Ron *"Reasserting the Vision /Mission of Black Nationalism: Remembering Malcom in a Time of Crisis"* Institute of The Black World." Available from http://ibw21.org/vantage-pont/reasserting-the-vision-mission-of-black-nationalism-rembering-malcom-in-a-time-of-crisis (accessed July 2015).

Day, Katie, *Faith on the Avenue*, New York, NY: Oxford University Press, 2014

Dudley, Carl S. Effective Small Churches in the Twenty-first Century. Nashville, TN: Abington Press, 2003.

Early Childhood Partnerships: Available from: http://www.heinz.org/userfiles/library/execsum-final.pfd (accessed February 2016).

Education Legislation: Available from: http://www2.ed.gov/policy/landing.jhtml (accessed February 2016).

Ellison, Craig W. *The Urban Mission*, Grand Rapids, MI: William B. Eerdmans Pub. Co, 1974.

Feeney, Jim, *"Small Churches Please God, Too: Sermons on The Church."*

Available from http://www.jimfeeney.org/small-churches.html (accessed September 18th, 2014).

Franklin, Robert M. *Crisis In The Village: Restoring Hope in African American Communities* (Minneapolis, MN: Fortress Press, 2007.

Gibbs, Eddie, *Church Next*, Madison, WI: Intervarsity Press, 2000.

Giles, Kevin. *"House Churches."* Winter, Vol.24, no.1. Available from www.cbeinternational.org/sites/default/files/houseGiles. pfd (accessed November 2015).

Guder, Darrell L. *Missional Church: A Vision for sending the church in North America*

Grand Rapids, MI: Eerdmans Publishing, 1998.

Gross, Edward N. *Are You a Christian or a Disciple?* United States of America: Xulon Press, 2014.

Hibbert, Richard Y. "The place of church planting in mission: Toward a theological Framework." *Evangelical Review of Theology*, ERT (2009):33 (4): 316-331.

Hill, Kenneth H. *Religious Education in The African American Tradition* Danvers, MA, Chalice Press, 2007.

Hong, Stephen. "Reversing A Downward Spiral: Strengthening The Church's Community, Holiness and Unity Through Intentional Discipleship," Asian Journal of Pentecostal Studies 15:1 (2012): 92.

Hunt, Joel R.E. *Thy Kingdom Come.* Augustana Book Concern, 1920.

Jacobson, Rolf A. "The Lord is God of Justice" (Isaiah 30:18) The Prophetic Insistence on Justice in Social Context. *Word & World* Vol 30, No.2, (Spring 2010), 125.

KCA Mission: Available from: www.christbiblefellowshipministries. com (accessed February 2016).

Kitchens, Jim, *The Postmodern Parish: New Ministry for a New Era.* Bethesda, MI: Alban Institute, 2003.

Kloetzli, Walter and Arthur Hillman, *Urban Church Planning,* Philadelphia, PA: Muhlenberg Press, 1958.

Kotter, John P. *Leading Change.* Washington, DC: Library of Congress, 2012.

Lund, Gordon C. *Thy Kingdom Come,* Philadelphia, PA: Muhlenberg Press, 1958.

MacIlvaine III, Rodman W. "What Is The Missional Church Movement?" Bibliotheca Sacra 167 (January -March 2010):89-106

Mantone, Amanda, "Storefront Churches Are a Lifeblood to Urban Poor." The Christian Century, Vol 121, Issue 8. http://www.questia.com/read/1G1-115833952/storefront-churches-are-lifeblood-to-urban-poor (accessed April 8, 2015).

May, Douglas C. "Why Are There Small Churches?" Concordia Theological Quarterly Vol 67: 1(January 2003): 87. www.ctsfw.net/media/pdfs/CTQTheologicalobserver67-1pfd. (accessed April 02, 2015).

McKnight, Scot, *A Community Call Atonement.* Nashville, TN: Abington Press, 2007.

McKnight, Scot, *The Jesus Creed.* Brewster, MA: Paraclete Press, 2004.

McNeal, Reggie, *Missional Renaissance.* San Francisco, CA: Jossey-Bass Publishers, 2009.

Medicating ADHD: Too much? Too Soon? Available from: http://www.apa.org/monitor/dec01/medicating.aspx (accessed February 2016).

Meyers, Eleanor, Scott, *Envisioning The New City.* Louisville, Kentucky: John Knox Press, 1992.

Mott, Stephen, Slider, Ronald, J. "Economic Justice: biblical paradigm" Transformation (April 2000): 50.

NCAA, Probability of competing in sports beyond high school: Available from: http://www.ncaa.org/about/resources/research/probability-competing-beyond-high-school (accessed February 6, 2016).

Nelson, Peter K. "Discipleship Dissonance: Toward A Theology of Imperfection Amidst the Pursuit of Holiness" Journal of Spiritual Formation & Soul Care, *VOL.4*, No 1, (2011): 63-92.

O'Brien, Brandon. *The Strategically Small Church*, Minneapolis, MN: Bethany House Publishers, 2010

Ortiz, Juan C. *Call To Discipleship*, Plainfield, NJ: Logos International, 1975.

Pappas, Anthony G. *Inside The Small Church*, Herndon, VA: Alban Institute Publishers, 2002.

Perkins, John M. Beyond Charity: *The Call to Christian Community Development.* Grand, Rapids: MI: Baker Books Publishers, 1993.

Philadelphia School District, Available from: http://articles.philly.com/2011-05-01/news/29493380-1-full-day-kindergarten-half-day-kindergarten-block-grant. (accessed

February 2016).

Providence Theological Seminary Blog: *On Christotelic-Hermeneutics.* Available from http://nct-blog-ptsco.org/2012/09/03/christotelic-hermeneutics-part1/ (accessed February 6, 2016).

Ray, David R. *The Big Small Church Book*, Cleveland, OH: Pilgrim Press, 1992

Razor, Stephen C and Christine D. Chapman, *Black Power From The Pew: Laity Connecting Congregations and Communities*, Cleveland, Ohio: The Pilgrim Press, 2007.

Ridderbos, *The Coming of the Kingdom*, trans. H. de Jongste Philadelphia: The Presbyterian and Reformed Publishing Company, 1976.

Rouse, Rick and Van Gelder, Craig, A *Filed Guide for The Missional Congregation* Minneapolis, MN: Augsburg Fortress Press, 2008.

Roxburgh, Allen J. and Romanuk, Fred. *The Missional Leader* San Francisco, CA: Jossey-Bass, 2006.

Sarisky, Darren. "The Meaning of the mission Dei: Reflections on Lesslie Newbigin's Proposal That Mission Is of the Essence of the Church" Missiology: *An International Review*, Vol 42(3) (2014): 257-270.

Schaller, Lyle E. *Small Congregation Big Potential*

Nashville, TN: Abington Press, 2003.

Schrock, Simon. *One Anothering*, Green Forest, AR: New Leaf Press, 1991.

Smith, Daniel P. and Sellon, Mary, *Pathways to Renewal*. Herndon, VA: The Alban Institute, 2008.

Sunday Schools: Available from: http://www.encyclopedia.com/topic/Sundayschool.aspx (accessed February 2016).

Surge, Thomas J. *Origins of the Union Crisis, Race and inequality in Postwar Detroit*. Princeton, NJ: Princeton University Press, 1996.

Terry, John M. "The Small Church Overseas." Review and Expositor, 93 (1996): 383

The Baptist Union of Great Britain, *"Small Churches Project. Report to Council."* Available from http://easternbaptist.org.uk/files/smallchurchBU.pfd (accessed May 14, 2015).

The Kensington Neighborhood of Philadelphia: A Neighborhood Divided. Available from http://kensingtonphiladelphia.wordpress.com/ (accessed February 2016).

Walvoord, John F. and Zuck, Roy B. *The Bible Knowledge Commentary: New Testament Edition*, Eastbourne, England: Chariot Victor Publishing, 1983.

Wimberley, Edward P. *African American Pastoral Care*, Nashville TN: Abingdon Press, 2008.

About the Author:

D r. Michael D. Wright Sr is an alumni of Biblical Theology Seminary in Pennsylvania, receiving a Master's of Divinity, with a concentration in Urban Missional Theology. He is also a graduate of the Lutheran Theological Seminary of Philadelphia, earning a Doctorate in Ministry, with a concentration in Black Church Studies. Dr. Wright is the founder of the Christ Bible Fellowship Church of Philadelphia, located in Philadelphia, Pennsylvania, where he serves as the Senior Pastor/ Teacher, and the CEO of the Kensington Christian Academy. As a bivocational pastor, Dr. Wright has served the Philadelphia Fire Department for the past twenty years, first as a decorated Paramedic, and currently as the Director of the Employees' Assistance Program. Dr. Wright and his wife Lynne watched the providence of God move in their lives as they planted the Christ Bible Fellowship Church in their home, then moving to a storefront ministry, and finally transitioned into a permanent location, where they started the Kensington Christian Academy. Dr. Wright and his wife Lynne continue to grow the ministry as they follow God into the trenches of the urban community. Dr. Wright and his wife Lynne, have been married for thirty-four years, and have four children, and thirteen grandchildren. In his spare time, he enjoys traveling; reading; music; and photography.

CPSIA information can be obtained at www.ICGtesting.com
Printed in the USA
BVOW06s0933210716

456105BV00006B/9/P

9 781498 473576